The Fighter's Guide to Divorce

A no-holds-barred strategy for coming out ahead

The Fighter's Guide to Divorce

A no-holds-barred strategy for coming out ahead

Robert Blackwell

Contemporary Books, Inc.
Chicago

Published by Contemporary Books, Inc.
180 North Michigan Avenue, Chicago, Illinois 60601
Manufactured in the United States of America
Library of Congress Catalog Card Number: 79-51515
International Standard Book Number: 0-8092-8004-3 (cloth)
0-8092-7138-9 (paper)

Published simultaneously in Canada by
Beaverbooks
953 Dillingham Road
Pickering, Ontario L1W 1Z7
Canada

To Beth and Bob, the loves of my life,
and to the late Mrs. Esther Kagan,
and to all the parents in the world
who love their children and want them.
They were my inspiration.

Contents

Acknowledgments

This book could not have been written had I not enjoyed the confidence and cooperation of hundreds of attorneys, ministers, priests, rabbis, social workers, child and school psychologists, private investigators and literally thousands of divorced and separated persons. For the most part, these helpful individuals remain unidentified because that was my commitment to them. The accounts of their experiences have been modified to preclude any possibility of identification, but not sufficiently to change the substance of the points that they illustrate.

All of those I interviewed provided information, insight, and encouragement, but I am particularly grateful to some fine attorneys—Caryl P. Bonotto, Stanley F. Kaplan, and William C. MacLean of Chicago, and the late Garland C. Boothe, Sr., of Scotch Plains, N.J.; to The Honorable Charles J. Fleck, presiding judge of the Domestic Relations Division of Cook County, Illinois, Circuit Court; to Gene Allen of E.V. Allen and Associates, Inc.; to Phil Drotning for his assistance in editing the final manuscript; and to the late Mrs. Esther Kagan, who supplied brilliant advice and moral support during the seven years I devoted to the book.

Introduction

Nearly two centuries ago Alfred, Lord Tennyson, wrote that "marriages are born in Heaven." Today, a less romantic poet would probably concede that too often they end in Hell.

A combination of forces—women's lib, the erosion of doctrinaire Catholicism, the destigmatization of divorce—are steadily increasing the odds that a marriage will not endure. More than one million marriages were dissolved in 1975, but even that shocking figure does not reflect adequately the mounting rate of divorce in our society. Perhaps a more realistic measure is found in the statistics from Cook County, Illinois, where, in 1978, 45,790 marriage applications were filed and 29,790 persons filed suit for divorce.

The increasing fragility of matrimony suggests that, if you are now married, there is a 50-50 chance it won't last until death do you part. If you are sued for divorce and aren't prepared for the confrontation, the probability is even greater that you will lose more than your spouse. Particularly, if you are male, you could lose your children, your insurance and investments, and also your house.

What we have euphemistically come to call "civilized man"—a creature rarely found in divorce courts—has long considered the family to be the cornerstone of a stable society. It follows that, if our society is built on marriage, then divorce is a tragedy for more than those directly involved. It is a misfortune for the total society, as well.

Subjectively, there are no victors when a marriage ends in divorce; there are only victims. Whether the judge finds for the plaintiff or for the defendant, both will surrender to their attorneys a substantial portion of the assets that were theirs before the union was dissolved. One of them will almost certainly lose the children. And the children, who will lose the comfort, security and support of a normal family structure, will be the greatest losers of all. On them will be visited a disaster that, like their very presence on earth, was the sole creation of their parents.

Clearly, a suit for divorce is not an action to be taken lightly but one to be avoided if less drastic solutions can be found. Yet, often it may be the only realistic choice. In that event, the rational objective should be to accomplish it in a mature and responsible manner. But that is easier said than done.

Much of the trauma that attends the termination of a marriage is the product of a legal system that is basically adversary and requires that one of the parties to the divorce be found innocent and the other guilty. This is true even in "no-fault" states when it comes to settlement terms. The need to find one person responsible for the failure of a marriage creates much of the bitterness, the hostility and the deception that are standard ingredients of the divorce process.

Even in cases where the parties involved have enough surviving good will or trust in each other to believe the marriage can be terminated amicably, it rarely happens. By the time the opposing attorneys have finished coaching their clients, all signs of amity probably will have vanished.

It is my hope that this book will save some marriages by exposing the ugly consequences of a decision to divorce. Many marriages can be preserved, even happily, if the partners are strongly motivated to try. Failing that, I would hope that a better understanding of the legal processes involved, and of the destructive role often played by one or both attorneys, will circumvent the unnecessary rancor and bitterness that so often emerges when otherwise nice people decide to part.

An unselfish couple will recognize that the consequences of a bitter and protracted legal battle are not a cross to be borne exclusively by the litigants. If children are involved, it is virtually impossible to terminate the relationship so conclusively that further social intercourse is not required—in fact, desired—by many of the parties involved. A marriage of any duration usually will have generated close friendships between more than one generation of two families. It is desperately unfair to force friends and relatives to choose sides in a conflict that was not of their making, and despicable to visit such a choice upon the children. Yet, this often happens when the emotional and psychological impact of a fiercely contested divorce action overcomes reason and compassion and provokes vindictive and irresponsible behavior by one or both of the parties.

Beyond these concerns, which are paramount, I am also painfully aware of the needless tragic consequences endured by literally thousands of defendants, male and female, who have been the victims of an insidious legal process that enriches lawyers and often impoverishes their clients.

Too often, the product of the divorce lawyer's vineyard is bitter wine for the client. There are lawyers whose only interest in the proceeding is the amount of their fee; there are devious lawyers, dishonest lawyers, incompetent lawyers; there are inexperienced and indifferent judges and others whose case loads preclude more than cursory examination of the evidence, and a judgment based on instinct, emotion or prejudice, rather than on a thoughtful and rational evaluation of the facts.

The author, happily, is not an attorney. If I were, I would be too busy separating confused and distraught litigants from their assets and from each other to waste highly profitable hours writing a book. But in seven years of dealing with divorce attorneys in my own behalf and in behalf of hundreds of others who have come to me for help, I have developed enormous respect for competent, ethical attorneys—and unmitigated disgust for the rapacious ones. Unfortunately, the divorce specialty has more than its share of the latter, who are nothing more than legal predators.

If you have been sued for divorce, you should assume (although it may not be the case) that your spouse has a skilled and heartless attorney in his or her corner. If the stakes are sufficiently high, and the rancor and bitterness sufficiently deep, they may already be mustering their minions for the offense—private detectives, photographers, electronic wizards, hostile witnesses—with the ultimate objective of destroying your reputation and your credibility. They may try to entrap you. They may even suborn perjury against you.

However well you thought you knew your spouse, remember he or she may now be receiving expert instruction in the martial arts of divorce. Don't expect mercy. Don't even expect fair play. This is one contest that escaped the attention of the Marquis of Queensberry. Divorce is a dirty business, and, more often than not, "dirty" is the way the game is played.

Almost inevitably, the settlement in your divorce action will affect you for the rest of your life. It may determine whether you can live in reasonable comfort, whether it is feasible for you to remarry, whether you can see your children. It is worth a substantial investment of time, energy and ingenuity to ensure that you negotiate the best possible terms. The more you know about divorce laws and procedures, and the more care you exercise in the selection of your attorney, the better will be your chances of escaping an emotional and financial disaster. If you don't learn how to defend yourself, you will have only yourself to blame if you are separated permanently from your children and your assets, burdened with unconscionable future payments and saddled with all of the accumulated debts.

Whether you decide to initiate divorce proceedings or your mate decides to institute them against you, this book will help you to prepare for what probably will be the battle of your life. The information it contains is based on my own experiences and more than four thousand interviews with men and women who know the hazards of divorce firsthand. Many of them have endured unspeakable indignities at the hands of unscrupulous lawyers, indifferent judges and vindictive mates. Other material has been gathered from scores of attorneys, judges, clerics and private investigators. Much of this information may tax your credulity if you are preoccupied with the trauma of a bad marriage and have yet to be exposed to the barbarous tactics often employed in and out of court.

Let me assure you, though, the hazards and pitfalls I describe are real. All of them have been experienced by hapless victims of our heartless and often savage divorce procedures. You should be aware of them so you will be prepared to defend yourself. Yet, don't let yourself become paranoid about what lies ahead. You need to keep your cool, and it isn't likely that everything in this chamber of horrors will happen to you.

Likewise, the precautions and remedies prescribed are not meant to apply in all situations. Your doctor doesn't empty his medicine cabinet to treat every ill. He diagnoses the ailment and prescribes the medicine that will effect the cure. You, too, should make a continuing diagnosis of your own unique divorce situation and be selective in using the medicine that is prescribed.

Because one of the objectives is to help you select a competent attorney, I have dwelt on examples of the kind of legal counsel you should avoid. Do not infer that a majority of lawyers fall into this category. In my own case, I was blessed with honest, capable, and understanding legal counsel. You can be, too, if you take the precautions I will outline.

Finally, *The Fighter's Guide to Divorce* is intended to help you make sound decisions during a trying period that will profoundly affect your future. It can be a valuable ally if you use it wisely, but it is most emphatically *not* intended as a substitute for sound professional legal advice. You will need the best lawyer you can find.

I hope you find him, or her.

1

Some Things You Should Consider Before You See Your Lawyer

PERHAPS, during your years together, you and your partner have grown apart and now have so little in common that your marriage doesn't make sense anymore. Or you may have discovered you are genuinely incompatible and that your eternal bickering is destroying you and also your children. Possibly you are at your wit's end because your wife is bankrupting you with her extravagance or your husband is demeaning you with his parsimony. Perhaps your husband is overbearing and abusive or your wife is a nag and a shrew. Maybe one of you is insanely jealous, or alcoholic, or unbearably dull. Possibly you disagree over the rearing of your children, or haven't had any and want some, or are frustrated because your sexual relations are unfulfilling. Perhaps you have simply decided that there is more to life that you are missing. Conceivably, you or your spouse may already have found the person with whom that new and more rewarding life will be shared.

Whatever your reasons, you have decided you and your spouse can no longer live together, or your spouse has made that decision, or both of you have.

If you were Moslems, the solution would be immediate and uncomplicated. The husband would simply announce to his wife, "I divorce thee, I divorce thee, I divorce thee," and the marriage would be permanently and irrevocably dissolved. In much of Africa, a simple declaration by the husband would also suffice. In China or Japan, a divorce could be accomplished by mutual consent, and in other nations with the approval of your family or your church.

But in most of the Christian nations, the termination of a marriage is a much more onerous, complex, and costly process. Prior to the Declaration of Independence, the American colonies were restricted by the British marriage laws, which then required an Act of Parliament to sanction a divorce. The effect, in Britain, was to limit divorces to two or three a year, usually involving members of the nobility. Although the colonies were only slightly more liberal, they were too lenient to please King George. In 1772, incensed because the Pennsylvania assembly granted a Philadelphia barber a divorce from his adulterous wife, the King prohibited provincial governors from granting divorces "upon any pretense whatsoever."

With this sort of heritage, laws governing divorce in the United States evolved with the grounds severely limited and the legal mechanisms increasingly complex. Today, a couple desiring to divorce is confronted with a cumbersome legal process controlled by the state, presided over by judges, and contorted by lawyers to enhance the financial rewards of their profession. One might note that only in the legal profession are profits generated in inverse proportion to productivity.

However convinced you may be that divorce is the only solution to your problems, prudence demands that you approach it with caution. Collect your wits and ponder a few important questions before you ensnare yourself in a legal web that many others have discovered can be painful, degrading, and costly.

You would do well to begin by asking yourself whether you are too upset and distraught to make a rational decision. Have you exhausted all of the less drastic alternatives: a visit to your spiritual advisor or a marriage counselor, for example? Could your marriage be annulled? Would a legal separation make sense, to give you time to consider whether you really want to terminate your marriage finally and forever? Do you have grounds for divorce, or does your spouse have more than you have? Can you afford a divorce? If you can, whom will you engage as your lawyer? Will you be able to protect your assets from your spouse and the lawyers?

Most important, have you considered your children? Have you looked with understanding and compassion at the traumatic impact the division of your household will have on them? Have you asked yourself whether your own desire to escape what seems to be an intolerable situation gives you the right to inflict what may be an even less tolerable situation on your offspring, who love and need both of their parents? If you are a man, do you really want to risk losing your children to obtain a divorce? Remember, judges are almost always inclined to give custody to the mother, even though she may be the less stable and responsible of the parents.

These are only a few of the questions you should try to resolve before you consult a lawyer. As you read this book, you will think of others. Don't try to evade them or respond to them with rationalizations. You have a lot at stake and, once you have engaged an attorney, the odds are there will be no turning back. Unless you retain a remarkably ethical and high-principled attorney, he or she will see to that.

Let's assume you are willing, for the moment at least, to take my advice. You want to enter this disquieting new chapter of your life with your eyes open and your feet planted firmly on the ground. What do you need to know?

What Are the Grounds for Divorce?

Your place of residence will determine the grounds for divorce available to you.[1] They are narrowly restricted in some states; in others, particularly the "no-fault" states, they are quite liberal. As this is written, about forty states have adopted "no-fault" divorce laws, permitting couples to part legally on grounds of irreconcilable differences, without requiring that blame be fixed on one party or the other. However, the process is not as neat as it may seem, for even in the "no-fault" states the grounds for dissolution of the marriage become important in the division of property, granting of child custody, and determination of alimony.

What about the states that have not adopted "no-fault" laws? In these jurisdictions, some of the most common grounds for divorce are:

Mental cruelty
Physical cruelty
Desertion
Fraud
Insanity
Underage
Impotence
Incompatibility
Incapacity to contract a legal marriage
Adultery
Bigamy
Duress
Habitual drunkenness
Failure to support
Incest
Conviction of a felony
Drug Addiction
Communication of a social disease to a spouse

Ultimately, if you decide to proceed with a divorce action, you and your attorney will have to consider what grounds you have and, more important, to determine which of them you can reasonably expect to prove. You will save time and money (in legal actions, time *is* money) if you learn how these grounds are defined and consider them in the light of your own marital experience. And be honest with yourself. Don't limit these explorations to the grounds you believe you may have; also consider those that might be put forth by your spouse in a countersuit against you. It is not unusual for the spouse who performs this exercise honestly and diligently to discover that the other party to the marriage is, in fact, the more aggrieved of the two. In any event, this preliminary effort on your part will be helpful when you finally meet with your lawyer. It should also reduce his fee, for you will probably be paying him by the hour.

Most of the grounds for divorce cited here are self-explanatory, but some of the most common ones require further definition. As you read these definitions you might begin to list conditions or events in your own marriage that seem to fit the description so you will be prepared to discuss them with your attorney.

Mental or Physical Cruelty

This is an attempt to injure the mental or physical well-being of the mate. Inadvertent or unintended acts of cruelty do not constitute grounds: there must be proof the cruelty was deliberate.

In mental cruelty cases, there must be proof of a malevolent motive and intention. Verbal threats that make you fear for your life often may be sufficient evidence of mental cruelty—if you are able to prove they were made.

In physical cruelty cases, the act of violence alone usually implies the malevolent motive and intent to harm. However, the circumstances of the violent act must preclude the possibility that the injury was accidental rather than deliberate, and actual physical injury—or the threat of it—must be shown.

The acts supporting a charge of mental cruelty often are broadly defined. The following excerpt from a divorce complaint on file in the Circuit Court of Lake County, Illinois, illustrates how broad they can be.

> 5. That during all of the time that the parties lived together as husband and wife, the Plaintiff conducted herself as a good, true and faithful wife toward the defendant.
>
> 6. That the defendant, wholly regardless of his marriage covenants, vows and obligations as a husband, has for a long period of time prior hereto been guilty of extreme mental cruelty toward the Plaintiff, in that he has, by his actions and conduct toward her, wrongfully inflicted upon her great and grievous mental pain, suffering and anguish, and the Plaintiff alleges that the following are some instances of such mental cruelty which occurred during the period of the marriage of the Plaintiff and the Defendant:
>
> A. Treated her with extreme coldness and indifference, and frequently refused to carry on any discussions with her when she attempted to discuss with him matters of vital importance to their family relationship
>
> B. Refused her the normal companionship of a husband by willfully refusing to converse with her for long periods of time and to engage in any social activities with the Plaintiff, thereby causing her to lead a lonely and unhappy existence.
>
> C. Refused, despite her numerous pleas and requests, to assist

her in assuming any of the routine household chores and responsibilities, and advised the Plaintiff to hire household help, but when she did hire such outside cleaning help, he would become angry and disturbed with her for wasting money on such help; that such conduct on the part of the Defendant resulted in the Plaintiff not only having the sole responsibility for taking care of the Three (3) minor children of the parties, but also to clean and maintain the marital residence of the parties when the Defendant was well able financially to afford the Plaintiff some assistance in regard to the foregoing.

D. Displayed a total lack of warmth and feeling in his relationship to the Plaintiff and was only interested in a physical relationship with the Plaintiff to the exclusion of any emotional involvement in (the) relationship so as to deny to the Plaintiff the normal love and companionship of married life.

E. Constantly criticized the Plaintiff in the manner in which she cared for the Three (3) minor children of the parties, even though he himself never offered to assume or even share with her the responsibility for the care of the said children; that he told her on numerous occasions that she was mentally ill and that she was unfit to care for the children, but again refused to share with her the responsibilities involved in the care and maintenance of their children.

F. That he is continually, on those infrequent occasions, when he finds time to converse with the Plaintiff, verbally abusive toward her and is argumentative over matters and issues of relative unimportance.

7. That all of the aforesaid conduct of the Defendant, and all of his said acts, were wholly without cause or provocation on the part of the Plaintiff, and have caused her grievous mental and physical suffering, humiliation and unhappiness and have caused the marriage of the parties to become intolerable to the Plaintiff. . . .

The court in this case found for the plaintiff, demonstrating that in some courts, at least, a lack of social life and the absence of social discourse between husband and wife can be mental cruelty, as can the lack of an intimate physical relationship, verbal abuse, and many other causes of marital unhappiness. He lost custody of his children and many of his physical assets, and was ordered to pay his ex-wife $100 a month alimony in gross and $100 for child support. She remarried less than four months after the decree was granted but under its terms he was required to pay alimony for three more years.

The defendant's strongest defense in a case such as this is either to disprove the allegations of cruelty or to prove that it was provoked by actions of the plaintiff and was not disproportionate to the provocation. Physical violence, however, will not be condoned by the court, even when provoked.

Adultery

This is a voluntary act of sexual intercourse with another who is not your spouse. Unless a spouse is terribly vindictive, he or she will probably resort to other grounds, because the charge is demeaning to the accuser as well as the accused and is a cruel burden to impose on the children. However, particularly in states where the grounds for divorce are severely restricted, it is a common complaint in divorce actions.

Spouses will often go to incredible lengths to establish grounds of adultery, including the use of private investigators and photographers to arrange the event—but I will get to that later. At this juncture, a couple of warnings will suffice. First, if you propose to accuse your spouse of adultery, be sure you can't be found guilty yourself. Second, spouses considering adultery as grounds for divorce should be wary of losing their grounds on the basis of condonation (forgiveness).

For example, let us suppose a husband has been guilty of adultery. His wife has discovered his infidelity and is ready to sue for divorce. However, before her intentions become public knowledge, they are invited by friends who are unaware of their marital difficulties to spend a weekend in the country.

During the overnight stay, the estranged mates share the same bedroom. The husband sleeps on the floor or in a chair, not in bed with his wife. When the weekend is over they leave, the host couple still unaware of their problems. Even though there was no sexual intercourse between the unhappy mates, the presumption is that there was, and the wife has negated her grounds for claiming adultery. Her action implies forgiveness for his straying ways.

Occasionally an injured wife, unaware of the implications of an act of condonation, is the victim of a plot by the husband to gain witnesses to an act of condonation. Take this case of a Midwestern man whose wife filed suit for divorce.

> My wife asked me if I would find a place to live separately for awhile, OK? So I moved out and the next day she ran and filed suit for divorce, which was a pretty sneaky thing and I've always disliked her for the fact that she wasn't honest about the whole thing.

Q. What grounds did she file on?
A. Adultery.
Q. She knew you were guilty of adultery?
A. Yes.
Q. Now, what was your plan to keep her from getting a divorce based on grounds of adultery?
A. To make it with her and have a witness. I made a deal with a friend of mine to be outside my window watching me make it with my wife.
Q. She didn't know he was there watching?
A. No, so she blew her own case right then. She went to her lawyer and he told her to drop the case. Her grounds for adultery were no good because she cohabited with me.
Q. What about your witness; did you have to pay him?
A. Oh, no, no, I just guaranteed him that if he ever needed help I would help him the same way.

Had the wife been aware of the plot, she might have salvaged her situation by filing a counterclaim that she had been victimized by her husband and his friend, negating her husband's claim of condonation.

Desertion

Desertion implies that a mate has left his spouse with no intention of returning. But desertion, as Daniel J. DeBenedictis warns in his helpful book, *The Legal Rights of Married Women,* may be difficult to prove.

"Remember," DeBenedictis writes, "you can't drive your

husband out of the house and then sue him for desertion. In this case, you would be guilty of desertion. The desertion must also be without your permission and consent or your case will be dismissed. Also, unless you can prove that your husband defrauded you (a difficult thing to prove), if you let him back into your bed and board for just one night, the required statutory (waiting) period[2] must start to accumulate all over again."

A wife may expect difficulty in sustaining a charge of desertion if, in the presence of witnesses, she has ordered her husband out of the house, threatened him with violence if he remains, otherwise made life intolerable for the purpose of causing him to leave or locked him out. Conversely, if she decides to go home to mama, it had better be because her husband drove her out.

Impotence

Impotence is legally construed as the inability of the husband to perform sexually. A husband capable of penetrating his wife, whether to her sexual satisfaction or not, is not impotent. The inability of the husband to stimulate an orgasm on the part of his wife, or even to produce children, does not constitute impotence.

The Legal Incapacity to Contract a Marriage

This can be present in numerous circumstances, the most frequent of which involve a mate who is underage, is pregnant by another at the time of marriage, or who perpetrates fraud or is guilty of bigamy or incest.

In your exploration of potential grounds for divorce, don't overlook the question: "Is my marriage legally valid?"

The presumption of legality favors ceremonial marriages. These are marriages performed in the presence of witnesses by ordained ministers, authorized civil officials, or the captain of a ship at sea who holds a valid license. If your marriage was performed by other means, your divorce may be a simple legal action instead of a gladiatorial contest.

Does checking these facts seem silly to you? Consider the

recent case in which a woman sued her actor husband for divorce and for one-fourth of the trust fund he was to receive from a relative. The couple had been married by an actor friend. The wife claimed the actor had declared he was an ordained minister. She questioned his capacity to perform the marriage.

Or suppose your husband or wife did not tell you until after your marriage that he or she had been married previously. This of itself may be grounds for divorce.

What About Legal Separation or Annulment?

A *legal separation* may be an intermediate step along the road to divorce court that is entered into by mutual agreement of the parties or, in some cases, it may be the result of a contested divorce where one partner fails to prove grounds. Accompanied by a separate-maintenance decree, it gives each spouse the right to live apart in relative freedom while also resolving the financial questions that would otherwise remain a bone of contention between them.

In some cases, the legal separation is simply a means of smoothing the paths of the warring partners as they negotiate the terms of the final decree. In others, it may provide a "cooling-off period," unmarred by financial disputes, during which they can decide whether they want their separation to be permanent. Occasionally it may be a permanent arrangement between two spouses who, for one reason or another, do not want to divorce.

For a wife, a separate maintenance decree is a method of assuring her right to support payments even though the couple is no longer living together as man and wife. Meanwhile, the husband can better manage his personal affairs because a fixed cost has been established for the maintenance of his wife and family.

Couples with a mutual desire to live apart, no desire to remarry, and the emotional stability to arrive at an equitable arrangement for support of the family may find a legal separation the least painful and costly solution to their problem.

Annulment is a legal procedure that declares that a valid

marriage never existed. Grounds for annulment vary from state to state but often include bigamy, impotency, fraud, underage, pregnancy at the time of marriage, or failure to consummate the marriage. If fraud was involved in contracting the marriage, the partner who perpetrated the fraud cannot seek the annulment.

An annulment obtained under the civil law may preclude the wife from obtaining support payments. Thus, a husband seeking to avoid harsh alimony terms might prefer annulment to divorce, if he has grounds.

The more common form of annulment is that sought within the Roman Catholic church, following a civil divorce decree. The laws of the church do not prohibit divorce but do forbid remarriage of a divorced person who hasn't obtained an annulment. A divorced Catholic can receive the sacraments, but a divorced Catholic who has remarried without a church annulment cannot. Within the church, the "matrimonial court" is responsible for maintaining the literature and rules governing annulment and remarriage. The most common grounds for annulment are bigamy, impotency, psychological influences and psychic incapacity.

Under civil law, bigamy occurs when a second marriage is contracted without the formality of dissolving the first. The rules of the Roman Catholic church are more stringent, defining bigamy as a condition in which one remarries, even though divorced, while still having a living spouse. In a marriage that has been recognized as valid by the church, if it is discovered that one of the partners is a bigamist, the church may grant an annulment and permission to remarry to the innocent spouse.

Impotency, in the eyes of the church, is seen as the inability to fulfill the responsibilities of the marriage. It is recognized that, because of psychological factors, a husband may be impotent with one spouse, but not with another.

The vast majority of cases adjudicated in the matrimonial court involve psychological influences. Insanity or psychic incapacity *at the time of marriage* is grounds for annulment and permission to remarry

Many Catholics whose marriages have ended in divorce believe they must remain unmarried or leave the church if they wish to remarry. They should investigate the position of their parish priest or local archdiocese on annulment. Attitudes within the church have been liberalized considerably in recent years, and, if an annulment is possible, the procedure is relatively simple and the cost quite small.

The petitioner who has been granted a civil divorce and wants a church annulment fills out a number of forms supplied by the church. A preliminary investigation is made by a priest appointed to act as advocate for the petitioner. If the petition has merit, it is then formally investigated by a single judge or a panel of three judges. If the ruling favors the petitioner, it then must be reviewed by an official of the tribunal, known as the "defender of the bond." If he is not satisfied, he must require that the case be reviewed by the tribunal of another diocese. If satisfied, he may ask the archbishop to obtain permission from the National Conference of Bishops in the United States so that the annulment can be effective immediately. Church law also contains provisions for appeal.

In a classic Illinois case, a civil annulment was granted on the recommendation of a jury because the bride deceived her husband-to-be by providing him and the church with forged evidence that her first husband was no longer alive. Here is the husband's account of the episode.

> When Jane and I were dating and first thinking of marriage, she told me she had been married once before and divorced because he was cruel and insane. I explained to her that I was duty bound to the laws of the Catholic church and felt that marriage was forever. Subsequently, Jane told me her previous husband had, in his insanity, killed himself by driving around in the desert at speeds in excess of 100 m.p.h. until he smashed into something.
>
> I had no reason to doubt her at the time, and, since this made Jane a widow, not a divorcee, it allowed us to be married. She sat through instruction classes in preparation for joining the Catholic church. Two of those lectures described the rules for Christian marriage, and Jane claimed to understand those rules and regulations and agreed to abide by them.
>
> Subsequently, Jane showed me a death certificate she said had

> been supplied by a friend of the family who lived in a western state. I believed her and saw no reason to check it out. If she said he was dead, I believed her; if she said she had a death certificate, she had a death certificate. So far as I was concerned, the matter was closed.
>
> When Jane filed suit for divorce, I decided to check out her story and determine whether her first husband was really insane. She had been telling our friends I was cruel and insane, which was what she had told me about her first husband. I knew I wasn't cruel and insane and figured that if I wasn't, maybe he also wasn't—and maybe he also wasn't dead. I was determined to find out what the real facts were.
>
> I couldn't remember the name of her previous husband, so I called the state in which they were married and got his name and place of birth from their marriage license.
>
> Next, I obtained from directory assistance in his birthplace the phone numbers of everyone with the same last name and found, in one of the suburbs, a listing with the identical name. I called that number first and discovered that, while it was not the man I was trying to locate, it was his cousin. They had not seen each other for 15 years, but he gave me the name of the man's mother.
>
> She answered the phone when I called and was a very charming lady. I explained that I had married her son's ex-wife, believing her to be a widow, and that she was now divorcing me and accusing me of things that were not true. She expressed her sympathy and said she was sure her son, who was alive and well, would also be sympathetic. She gave me his telephone number.
>
> I dialed it and my wife's first husband came up out of his grave and answered the telephone.

That was only the beginning of the husband's search. Eventually, he tracked down a copy of the forged death certificate and noted that the husband's middle name was misspelled. He filed a suit for annulment, and when a deposition was taken from his wife, she was asked to spell her first husband's middle name. She misspelled it as it had been misspelled on the forged death certificate. Ultimately, with this evidence of fraud, the wife's suit for divorce was dismissed, and the annulment granted the husband. Three months later, however, the judge reversed himself and ruled the annulment unjustified under Illinois law. The decision was appealed. The Illinois State Supreme Court affirmed the Appellate Court's decision in 1979.

Do You Have to Prove Grounds?

As you review your own marital experience in the light of the grounds for divorce I have described, it is imperative that you be as objective as possible, for guilt in a marital conflict is often difficult to ascribe. Your perception of an episode in your married life may be diametrically opposed to that of your spouse. If you allege misconduct on the part of your spouse as grounds for divorce, your attorney will want to have proof that the fault really lies with your husband or wife and not with you. Such caution is well-advised, for ultimately the discrepancies between your testimony and that of your spouse will be resolved by others, and if your perception of fault is distorted, your grounds for divorce may instead prove to be grounds for dismissal.

The grounds you allege are serious charges that may irreparably damage the reputation of your mate. If the action is contested and you cannot prove the grounds, you will lose the case. Yo may also expose yourself to a suit for malicious prosecution for making allegations against your spouse without probable cause.

It is not unusual for spouses with a mutual desire for divorce to concoct grounds in order to obtain a decree that otherwise would not be granted. In other cases, one spouse will make malicious false charges against the other, hoping they will not be contested. Each of these actions is immoral and unethical, and if you are tempted to take them you should consider carefully the potential consequences.

Keep in mind that the grounds for divorce, whether contested or not, become part of the trial's official record. Someday your children may want to investigate that record. Do you really want them to believe their mother or father was cruel or inhuman or an adulterer, if in fact that was not true?

Conversely, don't let your spouse's attorney frighten you into modifying your charges with the threat of publicity. "You don't want to see that in the papers," he or she might say.

Unless you enjoy the public stature of a sports figure or movie star, the possibility that the details of your divorce proceeding will appear in the newspapers is extremely remote. Odds are that there will be only a line or two about the final outcome, if that. With the divorce rate at its present level, newspapers simply do not have space to report divorce actions in detail, nor is there any real public interest unless the circumstances are dramatic and unique, or celebrities are involved. Beware, though, the possibility that if there are unique aspects to your case, a lawyer may tip off the press in order to secure publicity for himself.

Finally, if you are contemplating divorce, remember that it is as important to avoid giving grounds to your spouse as it is to find grounds for your own complaint. In most instances, settlements favor the faultless party.

One of my friends learned this too late. He thoughtlessly told his wife, in the presence of witnesses, that she could take her clothes and leave home. His chance remark became the basis for a charge of mental cruelty. His wife was granted a divorce and a settlement entitling her to 78 percent of his annual salary in alimony.

Remember also that even after a physical separation, your behavior may become the basis for charges against you. Inevitably, once a marriage has deteriorated to the point of physical separation, both parties become intensely aware of their own economic self-interest in the divorce proceedings that will probably ensue. In all probability, you and your spouse will begin a game of cat-and-mouse, each searching for evidence that can be used against the other.

There have been countless cases in which one spouse, faithful throughout marriage, became promiscuous after a physical separation occurred. By the time the divorce action reached the courts, sufficient evidence of adultery had been accumulated to produce a decree in behalf of the faultless party.

Even though you and your spouse are physically separated—even legally separated—be prudent about your behavior. Avoid soft lights and high fidelity in one corner of your apartment and infidelity in the other. If your spouse is monitoring that behavior, it may affect the divorce decree and the settlement terms you will be forced to accept.

Meanwhile, fight for your own future. If you suspect that your spouse is involved in an extramarital liaison, take whatever steps may be necessary—including the use of a private investigator—to gather the evidence you need to prove a charge of adultery in court.

An errant Midwestern friend of mine discovered too late that the wife he had dominated throughout their marriage had the courage to fight when her marriage was threatened. The man, a corporate executive, spent so much time in Washington, D.C., that his company maintained a permanent hotel suite for him there. He had a long succession of amorous playmates during his visits to Washington and finally met one he desperately wanted to marry. He filed suit against his wife, seeking a divorce on grounds of incompatibility and irreconcilable differences.

Not long after, while at work in his Washington office, he received a telephone call from the assistant manager of the hotel where he maintained his suite.

"I thought you would like to know that your wife arrived a few minutes ago and checked into your suite," the manager said.

The horrified husband caught a taxi and hurried back to his hotel. When he arrived in his suite, his wife was sitting calmly on the sofa. Spread out on the coffee table were assorted frilly underthings and sleepwear, a collection of incriminating love notes, and even an album of risqué photographs the husband and his paramour had taken of each other.

The determined wife, in her countersuit, took the husband for everything he had.

---

[1]Write your state attorney general to obtain a copy of the marriage and divorce laws in your state. A letter addressed by title to the state capitol should reach him.

---

[2]The statutory waiting period is that required by the state in order to prove desertion. Typically, it varies from one to three years.

2

Financial First Aid

DIVORCE, almost always a traumatic emotional experience, can also be the instrument of financial disaster for one spouse or both. Typically, the aggrieved spouse is so distraught that the marriage is perceived only as an intolerable personal relationship: the fact that it is also an economic partnership is ignored. Even couples with nothing else left in common do hold common assets. A major aspect of divorce proceedings is the division of those assets and the allocation of future income in the form of alimony or child support.

The ancient aphorism "Two can live as cheaply as one" was never valid, and with current income tax laws it is even less so today. Financial constraints become even greater when the assets are divided among two spouses and two divorce lawyers. However determined you may be to end your marriage, pause long enough to reflect on the financial consequences. It is almost inevitable that even the victor in divorce court will be worse off financially than he was before.

But let's assume you have decided to go through with it, or that your spouse is forcing you to, and that you have determined, as suggested in Chapter 1, that reconciliation is impossible. Your first thought should be to protect your assets, not only from your spouse but also from the lawyers who ultimately will be involved in the case.

Don't assume your mate is neither bent on vengeance nor smitten with greed. When the time comes for settlement, it will be a dog-eat-dog battle to determine who gets the larger share of the spoils—you, your spouse or the lawyers. Unless you have protected yourself—particularly if you are the husband—you may leave divorce court destitute, with all of your assets and much of your future income committed to your ex-mate. Very likely you will remain responsible for all past obligations and for the accumulated fees of your lawyer and your wife's, even though her income and assets are greater than yours. The lawyers' fees alone may be considerable. A friend of mine is now in court, defending himself in a suit brought by a divorce lawyer who is demanding a fee of nearly $30,000—and he lost the case!

It is difficult to be rational in the early, highly emotional stages of marital warfare. With all of the problems you have on your mind, the economic consequences of divorce may seem of minor concern. But let me assure you that, if you fail to take the proper precautions now, you will regret it later.

The following pages will offer a few pointers on what those precautions should be. Some of them may seem downright silly to you, in your present state of mind, but consider them anyway: when your marital surgery is performed, some preliminary first aid may prevent the court from amputating your assets.

Check Your Timing

It can be the best of times or the worst of times, from a financial perspective, to sue or to be sued for divorce. You may not be able to control the timing, if you are on the receiving end of a suit. But if you can, consider these suggestions.

If you are a woman, seeking a divorce when the family income is at a temporarily low ebb is probably not a wise move. Your alimony and child support payments may be based on your husband's present income. If you can stand living with the guy a little longer, delay acting until a time when the economy is on the upswing and your spouse again is reasonably affluent.

A man, on the other hand, should try to take advantage of a temporary setback in business and time his divorce actions for a period when his assets and income are reduced.

The time of year is important, too. Some couples, mutually desirous of an amicable divorce, wisely wait until after the New Year holiday before engaging legal counsel to manage their split. They know assets and income are often a factor in the setting of legal fees, and January is too early in the year to project the income of a salesman or self-employed person. This forces fee-hungry attorneys to accept income estimates for the new year. Even if the lawyer asks for the couple's previous income tax records, he cannot establish that they will repeat. He will have to accept their estimates for the current year.

Time of life can also be significant. One woman I know had been married nineteen years and six months when she was granted a divorce. Her lawyer failed to tell her she had to be married at least twenty years to qualify for her husband's Social Security benefits. Because of the attorney's negligence, she faces needlessly lean retirement years. The law has been amended to require only ten years of marriage to qualify.

Beware of Those Credit Cards

A primary concern in medical first aid is to stop the bleeding. To avoid being drained financially by a vengeful spouse, consider canceling all of your credit cards—those held singly by your mate as well as joint accounts.

How do you cancel a spouse's charge accounts after you are separated? Simply notify each store or company in writing, including the credit account number. You don't have to give a reason.

Instead of outright cancellation of joint accounts, husbands—primary holders of family cards—may wish to employ an alternative that will enable them to retain charge privileges for their own use. This can be achieved simply by reporting your credit cards as stolen and simultaneously requesting that new cards be issued with a change of address. The company will issue a new card with a different account number than the original, and it will be mailed to you at your new address. The old card becomes worthless, and only the new card is valid. This tactic has an added virtue. It may help you to avoid giving grounds for mental cruelty to your wife for deliberately denying her charge privileges.

Be sure, however, that you advise your wife of the action you have taken, explaining that your wallet was lost or stolen, and that you have cancelled all your cards. Tell her that, in view of your marital situation, you do not intend to obtain new ones for her. If you fail to notify her, she may be intercepted by department store security people, or even the police, when she tries to use her card. And you might be held responsible for the embarrassment you caused her.

If you have already filed for divorce, or your spouse has, don't wait for the decree before you cancel your credit accounts. Unscrupulous lawyers are not above advising their clients to dash off to Neiman-Marcus or Lord & Taylor and satisfy all of their long-felt desires for designer apparel and other luxuries. "Let him (or, less often, her) pay for it," they say. Divorce courts are replete with tales of spouses who took that advice, running up thousands of dollars in debts for which the more financially solvent spouse became responsible in the final settlement.

You might also consider publishing a legal notice disclaiming responsibility for your spouse's future obligations. This will not relieve you of responsibility for debts incurred by your wife to provide for her necessary expenses, but it could protect you in the event she incurs obligations in behalf of others, or for clearly frivolous purposes. Also, it may put a damper on her spending habits by warning potential creditors that, if they extend credit to her, they may have difficulty collecting their money.

Inventory Your Assets

The financial terms of your final settlement will be based upon an accurate survey of your assets. Husbands who feel entitled to some share of the household goods (after all, you're not going to live in a cave after the divorce becomes final) should make a careful record of joint household and personal effects.

Similarly, a cautious wife will also want such a record. In order to face her new life with a minimum reduction in her standard of living, she also should do some research on the status of the family's assets and income.

The most important source of financial data is the family's past income tax returns, whether filed individually or jointly. Wives not yet ready to reveal their desire for a divorce might surreptitiously photocopy these records. The prudent husband who suspects that divorce looms will try to prevent that by keeping all copies of past income tax returns in his possession. (You will discover later the importance of the tax return in revealing and obscuring financial assets.)

Another record to have handy when you arrive in post-decree court is a photostat of your wedding gift list. Which gift came from whose relatives could be important in determining the spouse to whom it will be awarded. That is, when you are bartering Aunt Matilda's Steuben glass vase for the radio that came from Uncle Henry, it will help if you can prove the radio really did come from your Uncle Henry. More about that later. Just take the time now to make this inventory, before the wedding gift list disappears or you lose access to it.

Next, take the time to inventory all the vast number of household items you have accumulated over the years. In bitterly contested divorce cases, treasured items often have a way of disappearing. An equitable final settlement may become grossly unfair when you discover that someone has absconded with a large portion of the items that were awarded to you.

You may be shocked one day, if you do not have such an inventory, to discover how much of what you thought you owned has disappeared. Early in 1971, one of my friends came home one snowy evening to discover that his wife, children, and furniture had vanished. Fortunately, he was able to trace both his family and his belongings. But if an item is missing and you cannot describe it accurately after your spouse has hidden it, sold it, or given it away, you might as well kiss it good-bye.

A simple inventory method is to take black-and-white and color photographs from several angles in each room of your house. Justify this action to your spouse as necessary in order to maintain a record of personal property for insurance purposes.

To ensure your ability to make absolute identification of your property in the future, you might also take advantage of the present drive by police departments to persuade families to mark their property with an electronic engraving pencil. In most cities, the police will lend you the instrument, with which you can inscribe your Social Security number on every valuable item. At the same time, of course, make a list.

Protect Your Household

Even though you may still be living in your home, burglars are not your only worry. As marital friction increases, friends and relatives may begin to make mysterious visits to your house or apartment. Their mission is to recover some particular item your spouse covets and cannot wait to get his or her hands on.

Have friendly neighbors keep an eye out for strange visitors to your home while you are away. Be suspicious of anyone who visits you claiming to be a salesman or pollster. Verify their identity by noting license plate numbers and checking with their supposed employers.

If belongings actually begin to disappear or you have indications you have had surreptitious visitors, confirm your suspicions by setting little traps to gather evidence of intruders. For example, if you keep the carpets freshly vacuumed, they will indicate footprints.

Ridiculous? Don't delude yourself. You are not concerned merely with protecting property. Your spouse or his or her investigators may be interested in matters more important than a favorite possession. They may be monitoring your activities, seeking evidence to support their grounds for divorce.

It could be awkward when a 36C bra turns up in court and your wife wears a 32A, or a size 34 pair of briefs is introduced as proof that your size 46 husband hasn't been the only man around.

Why, you may ask, not simply change the locks on the doors?

It sounds like an obvious solution, but your attorney may advise you not to do it, and for good reason. Let's suppose, for example, that you wish to prove desertion. Changing the locks may destroy that allegation because it denied your spouse the opportunity to return home.

In any event, if one locksmith can change your locks, another can make a key to fit them.

Finally, if you are the victim of surreptitious visits, gather all of the proof and witnesses you can, and keep careful notes. They may be helpful as your case develops.

Minimize Your Assets

Now that you have inventoried your belongings and taken steps to protect them, what about your more significant assets: stocks, bonds, bank accounts, real estate?

This is a treacherous area. Most of the actions you can take may have significant legal ramifications if you wait until after you have filed for divorce or have been served notice of a suit. It is one thing for a husband to shield assets from his wife. It's quite another to conceal them from a court of law. To be on the safe side, it would be wise to consult an attorney—but *not* the one you will retain for your divorce proceedings—and ask him to guide you through these actions. Chances are, your divorce lawyer will not risk a charge of unethical conduct by giving you this advice in anticipation of a legal suit. But even if he would, you don't want to risk a higher fee by exposing to him the full extent of your assets.

Many of the actions described in the pages that follow will be most useful to husbands, our society being what it is. But an alert wife will want to be aware of the possibilities, too. Women with independent income or inheritances should also consider several of the devices I outline.

Most important, when you see the first storm warnings, batten down your financial hatches. Do it while you still have legal freedom of action, before you file a divorce action or one is filed against you. It could mean the difference between future poverty and prosperity. Also increase the resources available to you while the divorce proceedings are in progress. Some lawyers urge their clients to try to retain control of as much as $10,000 in cash while the divorce proceedings are in progress.

Protect Your Cherished Possessions

Everyone has personal property that, although it may be of small financial value, is still cherished for sentimental or other reasons. Obviously, these are things you want to retain, but your spouse may have other ideas. One vindictive wife wouldn't allow her husband to keep a lovely ashtray given to him by his maternal grandmother. He gave her all the furnishings and the house, but she still wouldn't let him keep that ashtray. Another woman denied her husband the gold company watch he got from his boss on his 30th anniversary. A vindictive man refused his writer wife one source of her bread and butter—the research library she had accumulated over a period of twenty years.

If you believe you are up against a vindictive spouse—and by the time you reach court many spouses will be—consider selling some of your prized personal property now, before it is tied up in the estate and becomes part of the divorce settlement.

Sell? you ask. "Doesn't that defeat the whole purpose?" Not at all, if you have the cooperation of a trusted friend or relative.

Suppose you have some prized photographic equipment or a rare coin collection you value highly. If you act before any legal proceedings are instituted, you can legitimately sell them to a friend for a nominal amount and they will not become part of the spoils of your divorce. Just don't fail to keep a notarized bill of sale that will establish the date the transaction was executed.

After the divorce is finalized, you may repurchase your property at a slightly higher figure that will reward your friend for the use of his money. You will be able to retrieve your cameras, and they will provide you with potential ready cash should you need it. In all probability, you will.

Dispose of Your Automobile

In this mobile, car-conscious society, one of the first things your wife will want to get her hands on is the family automobile. Don't let her. Suppose she has an accident and others are killed or injured. You could be liable for thousands of dollars in damages.

But, even though you are able to retain the automobile while the divorce proceedings are in progress, you can be certain it will become a major prize in the property settlement, particularly if you own it free and clear.

Don't take any chances. Sell your present car and gain some more ready cash. Then buy a new one with the lowest down payment you can find. If your credit is good, your cash investment will be little or nothing; so little, in fact, that the lien will exceed the depreciated value of the car the minute you drive it out of the garage. Your wife isn't going to fight very hard for a car if all she wins is the privilege of paying off the note.

Don't Forget Form 1040

Your federal income tax return will be the prime source used by your lawyer and your spouse's to determine the extent and nature of your assets. It will reveal income from securities, rental property and royalties, as well as your salary and income from business or profession. A prudent man or woman will rearrange investments in order to reveal as little as possible on the federal tax form.

Investments in common or preferred stocks or industrial bonds will be revealed by interest or dividends reported on your federal tax return. This enables an accountant to calculate the approximate dollar assets that these investments represent. This knowledge, in the hands of a shrewd attorney for your spouse at settlement time, is as dangerous as a loaded gun, but there are several options that may help preserve your assets.

The first and most obvious is to dispose of your real estate and securities and hold the proceeds in cash. If you have a substantial estate, odds are that your opponent's attorney will tie up all your assets the minute they go to court. You will need cash desperately, so you might as well get your hands on it now. Unless your securities are jointly held, disposing of them will be no problem. Real estate presents a more complicated problem, and my best advice is to find a good attorney to assist you—one who can examine the manner in which the property is held and is intimately familiar with all the intricacies of the real estate laws in your state.

A real fighter who has witnessed the destitution of friends in divorce proceedings will sometimes go to any lengths, even illegal ones, to salvage assets. I know one man who, anticipating divorce proceedings, obtained, without his wife's knowledge, a $25,000 second mortgage on his house.

In the final divorce settlement he yielded the house to his wife in exchange for other concessions, without revealing the existence of the second mortgage. When the final decree was issued, he had the $25,000 and she had a house with two mortgages.

A second alternative, if you have already identified some of those who will ultimately share your estate, is to give some of your property away. But beware of gift tax implications. Gifts are taxed at three-fourths of the tax on the estate.

To avoid a gift tax, you can donate $3,000 annually to the same person and up to $30,000 to the same person in one lifetime exemption. But the lifetime exemption is cumulative. For example, a gift of $5,000 would mean that $3,000 could be deducted as an annual gift tax exemption, leaving $2,000 to be subtracted from the lifetime exemption.

If you don't wish to sell or give away your securities, consider switching your holdings to tax-exempt municipal bonds so that no dividends, interest or rental income will be revealed on your federal income tax returns. Although some municipals are in disrepute, many top-rated ones yield a good return.

(If your state requires that this income be reported, don't reveal the existence of the bonds on your federal return by taking the credit allowed for the state tax paid.)

If you are asked in court, under oath, about the ownership of municipal bonds, you will, of course, have to answer truthfully. But you don't have to volunteer the information. Let the federal return speak for itself, in the hope that your opponent's fee-hungry lawyer will be so eager to get on to his next case he will fail to ask you about items not revealed on your federal return.

Your investment in municipal bonds is protected further from the court's scrutiny if they are bearer bonds. Ownership of bearer bonds is not registered.

You may also conceal common stock ownership by investing in those which do not pay a cash dividend—long-range growth stocks or those that pay in stock splits.

Shelter Your Dividend Income

If you can't rearrange your investments, you can at least protect your access to the dividends as long as possible. Switch your mailing address for dividend checks, quarterly and annual reports and interim correspondence to a post office box or your office address. As an alternative, if the stocks are held jointly, you may be able to arrange with your bank to deposit dividend checks automatically to your joint checking or savings account. You, of course, will withdraw the cash promptly when the deposit has been made.

Loan Collateral

You may also retain control over part of your invested funds by using stocks or bonds as collateral for a loan. They then cannot be released until the loan is paid off. You, meanwhile, have gained access to more ready cash.

Checking and Savings Accounts

If you have joint accounts, clean them out before your spouse does.

Safe-Deposit Boxes

If you have a safe-deposit box to which you and your spouse have joint access—one containing cash, securities, or documents that will reveal the extent of your net worth—remove the contents while you still have the opportunity. If you haven't done so before you file your divorce action, or one is filed against you, your spouse probably will.

Some divorce attorneys employ the devious technique of advising their clients to clean out the safe-deposit box and then telling the spouse that this action has been taken. The instinctive reaction of the notified spouse is to dash to the bank to determine whether or not the box has, in fact, been emptied. Indeed it has, but the bank's records now indicate that the innocent spouse was the last person to have access to the deposit box, and can be presumed to have removed the contents. Certainly, at least, he or she can't prove otherwise.

If you do have cash or valuables you want to safeguard during the divorce proceedings, consider renting a deposit box out of state. If, through the methods already discussed, you have amassed a considerable sum in cash, you don't want to risk that it may be stolen. The same is true of those securities you have been unable to convert and other valuable documents to which you do not want your spouse to have access.

Be sure you use your own name on the box. You don't want to be accused of collusion or secretion. Don't reveal the existence of the box by having the statements sent to your home, and don't take the box rental as a deduction on your federal income tax. Also, avoid picking a bank in a city with which you are closely associated. Don't help your spouse's attorney find it if he or she decides to make a search.

Life Insurance

If you own life insurance in which your spouse is named as beneficiary, you may be sure an effort will be made to include in the final property settlement a requirement that it be maintained after the divorce without a change of beneficiary. If the policy has been in existence for some length of time, it probably has a substantial loan value on which you can borrow at a very low interest rate.

Borrow on it. It will reduce the value of the policy to your opponent if the final settlement requires you to maintain it and, meanwhile, you have generated more ready cash. Then change the beneficiary, perhaps to a trust for your children, so that, when you finally get to court, you won't own any life insurance naming your spouse as the beneficiary.

Your Will

If your spouse is the named beneficiary in your will, change it now, before any legal action is filed. In many cases, the courts have required, as part of the final settlement, that bequests made to the victorious plaintiff be maintained throughout the life of the losing defendant. Don't let this happen to you.

Even if that doesn't happen, don't risk the possibility that through oversight or carelessness you fail to change the beneficiary in your will after the divorce becomes final. There have been many cases in which one spouse or the other neglected to do so and years later the ex-spouse got the estate. Imagine the shock to the children of your second marriage if they are disinherited because you forgot to change your will, and your undeserving first spouse reaps the harvest of your lifetime of effort.

Trusts and Incorporation

One of the most distressing aspects of divorce, beyond the human emotional trauma involved, is the possibility you may lose control over those assets you have prudently and diligently accumulated over the years. Take action to minimize this prospect.

When you consult your attorney about changing your will, discuss the merits of putting real estate, business assets or stocks and bonds in a trust you can control. If you own your own business, such action may enable you to retain control over it after the divorce. A trust may also be a means of lowering your disposable income. The more you can reduce it, the less income will be available for alimony and child support when settlement time comes.

A trust can be a lifetime trust or run for a period of time. It can be irrevocable or subject to alteration or dissolution at your discretion. Any large trust company or major bank publishes samples of trust forms for attorneys, insurance agents and other interested persons. To be aware of the options, obtain copies of these forms and study them.

One form of trust that may be of particular interest is the sprinkling trust. You can bulk your assets in this trust, and the income from these assets is paid into a common trust fund upon which you have no claim.

The trustees of such a trust, named by you, determine to whom the income will be distributed, according to need. They may provide regular income to your children, or even pay you a salary as an employee of the trust. In any event, the allocation of the trust's income is "sprinkled" by the trustees and may go to different recipients from year to year.

It is unlikely that a spouse could break the terms of such a trust, unless he or she could prove an intent to defraud. This, again, makes it important that such an action precede the filing of a divorce action by either spouse.

Self-incorporation is another way to conserve your assets. You might, for example, incorporate yourself in the state of Delaware. You will hold the nonvoting shares and sell the voting shares to trusted relatives or friends. The nonvoting shares would be worthless to a vengeful spouse, should he or she attempt to sue for your assets in the corporation. A nonvoting shareholder cannot force dividends or control salaries, so you, through those who hold the voting shares, can determine the distribution of your future income.

Some Final Warnings

Caution your stockbrokers, investment advisers and trustees not to divulge any course of action you may have taken to protect and conserve your assets. A vengeful spouse who becomes aware of such actions may charge you with concealment.

Don't, in the process of safeguarding your assets, conduct business in any name other than your own. If you do, you risk being found guilty of secretion, which is comparable to fraud. This might create grounds for your spouse to claim that he or she has been deprived of assets to which a spouse was entitled. It also might contribute to a charge of mental cruelty.

Don't deal casually with the problem of safeguarding assets. Get the most competent legal advice you can find, but not from the attorney who will handle the divorce action itself. Remember, one of your objectives is to minimize his or her fee.

If you are a real fighter who is not yet in the divorce courts but sees storm warnings on the horizon, review your present financial arrangements with your spouse. Husbands should realize that the standard of living they allow their wives to maintain during marriage may be the standard the court will require them to sustain after divorce. If you have been unduly generous with your wife, now may be the time to pull in the reins. Poor-mouth your income and expenses and insist that personal spending be reduced.

In 1976, a Skokie, Illinois, woman appeared in divorce court demanding that, as part of a divorce settlement, her husband continue to maintain her in the style to which she was accustomed. She revealed to the judge that her wardrobe included: 60 purses, 92 pairs of slacks, 62 pantsuits, 106 blouses, 23 robes, 31 evening dresses, 86 pairs of shoes, 23 nightgowns, 55 body shirts, 47 slipovers, 39 sweaters, 27 vests, 25 halters, 87 necklaces, 36 bracelets and 10 watches.

The astonished judge dryly asked her if she was talking about the wardrobe in her house, or the one at I. Magnin—but the husband still paid dearly. The wife was awarded $700,000 over the next ten years and a $100,000 house. In addition to the provisions for the wife, the husband was also given responsibility for the support of his two college-aged daughters. Their wardrobes weren't itemized in court.

Finally, however adept you may be at investing in the stock market, the commodity market or real estate, take a vacation from these activities. Until your marital situation is resolved, the more liquid your assets are, the better off you will be. Moreover, you are going through the traumatic experience of separation or divorce—an emotional storm that may cloud your judgment. Wait. You'll be glad you did.

3

Choose The Best Lawyer You Can Find

TELEVISION attorneys like Perry Mason or Owen Marshall have a thoughtful, sympathetic, concerned appearance and manner that epitomizes integrity. Many divorce lawyers look that way, too. Your job is to be sure the qualities symbolized by your lawyer's appearance and manner are real, and that he or she is not wearing a convincing mask.

One of my friends, when sued for divorce, retained an attorney who, on the basis of appearance, could have won an Oscar as the movie version of a dedicated priest. He was sympathetic and understanding, and he gave every appearance of being honest, competent, and thoroughly professional.

As the legal maneuvering proceeded, my friend developed absolute confidence in his attorney and readily acquiesced when the lawyer advised him to give his wife a $50,000 settlement. "She's got too strong a case," he said. "If you settle now, you'll save money in the long run and avoid all the aggravation."

My friend signed the required documents. Five days later, his attorney married the now-affluent ex-wife, and the newlyweds honeymooned in Tanzania. You know whose money paid for their trip.

This example is not presented as typical of the behavior of most attorneys but, rather, to emphasize the need for caution in making your choice. Your case may be decided not in court but right now, by the quality and integrity of the attorney you select.

There are divorce lawyers who view their profession from the perspective of a shady used-car salesman, or an auto mechanic who, presented with a mechanically perfect automobile, will examine it and find a reason to charge you a hundred bucks. To some of these lawyers, the legal profession is not a sacred trust requiring the exercise of their highest skills but an assembly line operated for the purpose of separating you from your assets.

Dishonest attorneys are not above colluding with opposing counsel to negotiate an unfavorable settlement for their own clients in exchange for a share of the fee. It is a practice even more reprehensible than the fee splitting sometimes engaged in by physicians because, in that case, the patient does get rid of, say, his diseased appendix. In the case of divorce lawyers, the aggrieved client disposes of assets that should have been his.

One suburban Chicago woman was pressed by her attorney to accept a $75,000 cash settlement in lieu of alimony from a husband of substantial wealth. She stubbornly refused, and her attorney kept urging her to accept. Finally, disgusted, she discharged him and got a new lawyer. She learned subsequently from her former husband that her first lawyer had been promised a $7,500 side payment if he could get her to accept the $75,000 cash settlement that had been offered.

Another disillusioned woman offers the following, similar experience:

> I engaged an attorney to seek a legal separation, not a divorce, and for six months his fees kept building up while he tried to persuade me to forget about separation and file for divorce. Finally, in disgust, I dismissed him and changed to another firm. I had to pay his fees, of course, but at least I now had a lawyer I could trust.
>
> Shortly thereafter, my first lawyer's motives became clear. My

son informed me that my husband said he thought I had done the right thing because my first lawyer had repeatedly approached his lawyer offering to make "a deal" if he got me to settle for a cheap divorce. His proposal was that the two lawyers would then split the fee received from my husband for the money he saved.

If you eavesdrop on conversations between lawyers like these, you won't find them discussing the fine legal points of the case in which one of them is involved. More likely, one will be boasting, "Guess how much my new case is worth."

You can't afford an attorney who merely profits from your misfortune. You need one who will make a genuine effort to effect a reconciliation, if that seems advisable. Failing that, he will make a sincere and competent effort to help husbands and wives sever their legal ties efficiently and dispassionately, preserving, as well, enough financial and emotional equity to enable both of them to prepare for the future.

You won't find that kind of lawyer soliciting clients in the corridors of the local courthouse. You won't find him in a law firm that operates like a self-service discount department store. In all probability, you also won't find him in a huge corporate practice, however reputable it may be, because most of them shun divorce actions and have limited knowledge of current divorce law.

Finally, your lawyer won't be cheap. This is one time even the most inveterate bargain hunter should restrain those normal impulses. The finest attorney you can afford will be your best defense or offense in divorce court. You will do yourself no favor if you hire a cheap lawyer and emerge from court with an unnecessarily costly decree.

It may be, of course, that your financial circumstances make it impossible for you to engage a top-notch lawyer, or even any lawyer at all. If so, the option of pro se (for yourself) proceedings is open to you. But the aphorism that the person who acts as his own lawyer has a fool for a client also applies to divorce. Consider instead obtaining the assistance of your local legal aid society. Your local bar association can advise you of free legal assistance that may be available in your community.

After reviewing the tragic experience of literally hundreds of disheartened clients who were victims of rapacious or incompetent legal representation, I have developed seven rules that may guide you in your own search. Here they are.

Rule 1: Take Your Time

If your spouse beats you to the punch and a process server arrives with a subpoena, you will probably feel off balance and behind the eight ball. You may have taken seriously those words "until death do us part" and never contemplated the possibility of divorce. Perhaps you had assumed all was well with your marriage; you were preoccupied with your career and were unaware your spouse was overcome with boredom, or wounded pride, or were oblivious of the fact that late nights weren't really being spent at the office.

In any event, don't panic. Your instinctive reaction may be to dash off to the first lawyer you can find, but that is the least rational and most dangerous thing for you to do. The chances of your obtaining the representation you need and want are too remote if you are desperate.

If your spouse refuses to talk to you and hands you his or her lawyer's card with the suggestion that you talk to him, don't. If the lawyer calls you and wants to discuss the case, refuse to do so. If he is persistent, simply tell him that you are seeking counsel and that he will hear from your lawyer when one has been retained. Stall. Be calm. Don't divulge your plans to your mate or to his or her attorney.

Information thoughtlessly blurted out now may make it more difficult to fight your case later. An unwitting indication that certain settlement terms may be acceptable will give your spouse's lawyer a psychological advantage and could ultimately result in a more costly settlement than otherwise might have been obtained.

Rule 2: Research, Research, Research

Some people exercise more caution in buying a new automobile than they do in selecting a lawyer. If the car is a lemon, you can always trade it for another. If your lawyer proves to be a lemon, you could end up with outrageous alimony and support payments and be stuck with them for life. Your most important task now is to make certain you get the best lawyer you can find.

You don't want to find yourself in the position, as your case progresses, of one of my friends who failed to research his choice of lawyer.

> As the case progressed, it dawned on me that I was representing myself, rather than being represented by my lawyer. In the final stages, it was definitely me versus the opposing lawyer. I just didn't get the proper amount of encouragement and support from my lawyer. The other side constantly objected to statements I made, but my lawyers seemed unwilling to voice many objections to what was said by witnesses for my wife or by the opposing counsel.
>
> I finally suspected there was collusion between the two lawyers and started to fight for myself. I think the relationship between my wife's counsel, who is a matrimonial lawyer, and my counsel, also a matrimonial lawyer, is an unconscionable one. They were too friendly. I understand there is a national association of matrimonial lawyers. They sound like a plumber's union. The two lawyers did not, in my opinion, negotiate fairly in behalf of their clients. I did most of the negotiating, and, although I did better than my lawyer was doing, I didn't fare too well.

You might begin your research in a law office or law library by checking *Sullivan's Lawyer's Directory* for divorce law specialists in your city, or *Martindale-Hubbel Law Directory* for lawyers throughout the U.S. These references are used routinely by lawyers to contact other attorneys who specialize in a given field. Make a list of firms engaged in divorce practice. Ignore those that are not. Although the frequency of divorce has made this type of practice increasingly attractive, most major firms do not engage in it except where an important client is involved. Even then, they probably will engage an associate counsel who is a divorce specialist, understands the nuances of divorce law and is familiar with the most recent precedents and decisions. You are looking for a divorce lawyer, not a tax attorney—and one adept in trial work, if you believe your case will go to court.

Next, scout your area for organizations of divorced men and women. They may have information on file about local divorce attorneys. Ask them if they have a list of the "dirty dozen"—the local attorneys who specialize in dividing and conquering. These attorneys divide marital partnerships skillfully, but also they somehow manage to divide between themselves the couple's assets.

If you can obtain a "dirty dozen" list, cross those names from the master list you have prepared, but keep a record of who they are. Should you come up against one of them in court, forewarned is forearmed. If no such list is available, getting in touch with groups of people, or with as many individuals as you comfortably can, who have been divorced may enable you to compile a list of your own, based on their experiences.

Rule 3: Seek Advice

Ask other lawyers to recommend several competent, ethical firms who might represent you. Make it clear you are not considering their firm to handle your case but intend to retain someone who specializes in divorce work. Lawyers may impart more candid advice if they know they are excluded from consideration. If you already have an attorney or firm that represents you in other general legal work, this may be your best source of advice.

Avoid falling into the referral fee trap. Ask for several recommendations and don't reveal to the lawyer who is advising you which of these recommendations you intend to pursue. If the lawyer you select is obligated for a referral fee, you can be certain it won't be paid with his money. He'll get it from you.

Ex-clients may be an even more reliable source of information about the character, quality and integrity of your local attorneys and legal firms. How do you find ex-clients? It's time to go sleuthing again.

You have already sought out those people who are members of local groups of divorced persons. Now it is time to visit your local courthouse and check the divorce court docket for the previous year. It will provide the names of the attorneys in each case, the law firms involved and the names of the litigants. Make a list of the cases and the firms involved.

Next find the office in which the case records are maintained. You may be required to fill out a library call slip, but don't panic over this. Case files are a matter of public record you have a right to inspect.

Read through some of the cases. Look for examples that are similar to your situation, noting law firms and litigants that were involved. Try to observe which firms appear to have represented their clients most successfully.

Armed with the names of the litigants, it is now a simple matter to contact these fellow travelers along the road to divorce. Some people don't like to talk about religion. Others will consistently refuse to reveal their political choice. But almost anyone who has gone through the divorce mill is so uptight about the experience, your problem won't be getting him or her to talk about it. The problem will be turning off the tales.

Obviously, you will be well-advised to take nearly everything you hear with a grain of salt. Some of those you talk to will be obviously biased in their views. They may have developed a personal grudge against their lawyer for reasons quite unrelated to competence. Almost invariably, they will be extremely hostile toward the opposing counsel, but that isn't really what you are looking for. You want to know their attitude toward the attorney who represented them.

If you are a woman, telephone the wives who were represented by the finalists on your law firm list. Keep the conversation simple. Merely explain that you are about to become involved in a divorce action, are seeking an attorney, and want to avoid making an unfortunate choice. Tell each of them you are considering the firm that represented her and would like her opinion of it. She probably will tell you more than you really wanted to know.

If you are a man, contact the husbands who used the firms you have listed. If you have difficulty locating them, call the ex-wife. Tell her that her former husband owes you money;

she probably will be overjoyed to give you his new phone number and address, if he hasn't skipped altogether.

With the information you have gathered from other attorneys and ex-clients, your master list should be considerably reduced. You are almost ready to start interviewing prospective attorneys. But first review all of the information you have gained. Then observe Rule 4.

Rule 4. Know What to Look For

It is useful, in selecting an attorney, to understand what he or she can and cannot do for you. If your expectations are unrealistic or if they would require unethical conduct on the part of an attorney, now is the time to find out. It may spare you the expense of going through a drawn-out court action when the outcome is predictable and should have been resolved through a consent agreement rather than a costly trial. When you select your attorney, this knowledge may affect your choice.

Although not universally observed, the rules of behavior governing the conduct of the legal profession are quite precise. You can learn about them by visiting your local library and reading the American Bar Association's Canon of Ethics or Code of Professional Responsibility.

Next, make a list of your requirements.

a. You want an honest, competent attorney, not a predator, so you should be concerned about finding one whose first concern will be to satisfy himself that your marriage can't be saved, not the extent and liquidity of your assets.

b. You want a substantial, experienced firm, not a lone operator. A lone operator could become ill at the moment you need him most. He could lose or misfile papers. He could, during some periods, be so overburdened with work that none of his clients gets the attention and service that they deserve. I know of many cases that have been lost because an overworked or careless attorney failed to notify his client of a court appearance and, in his absence, the judge issued a decision favoring the other party. A large firm will be well-organized; it will have a "player on the bench" ready, if needed, who is able to substitute for the attorney assigned to your case.

c. Try to obtain the services of a senior partner in the firm (one with long experience in and out of court who has been exposed to most of the legal precedents), rather than a recent law school graduate who is just learning the ropes. Obviously, all lawyers must try cases to gain experience—but let them practice on someone else.

d. If you anticipate that your case will be tried in court, be sure you get a lawyer experienced in trial work: one who is articulate, understands judicial behavior, has the appearance of integrity and has a well-developed instinct in the art of jury selection.

e. You want a lawyer who is tough and uncompromising, one who will really fight for you rather than accept an easy settlement so he can collect his fee and get on with the next case. This is particularly important if you are somewhat irresolute yourself, because you will face some situations so distressing you may be tempted to yield just to get it over with. Get a lawyer who will do your fighting for you, even though you will also be fighting for yourself.

Rule 5. Don't Be Afraid to Shop Around

You are now ready to begin interviewing the prospective attorneys who remain on your list. Don't settle for the first one you talk to simply because he seems good enough. You may find a better one a block down the street. While selecting a lawyer isn't as impersonal as picking out a pound of peaches, good attorneys will not resent your shopping around. They know, for their sake as well as yours, it is important for you to find a lawyer with whom you can establish a good rapport, with whom you feel comfortable, whom you feel you can trust and who feels he can trust you.

Interview your final choices as carefully and incisively as you would an applicant for any other kind of work. Determine each counsel's batting average. Find out whether he or she has any obvious preference for representing men rather than women, or vice versa. Men will be best represented by attorneys who regularly pitch no-hit ball in a legal system that gives a conspicuous advantage to women. Women can expect a better settlement with the help of a lawyer who has an outstanding home run average in representing female clients.

During your interview, employ every device you can to judge the integrity of the candidate. Be tough. Your object is to select a lawyer who will not, because of avarice, incompetence, or indifference, sell you out. Try to determine if his typical strategy is aggressive or defensive, of if he has the wisdom, insight, and judgment to determine which strategy will be most effective in your case—and the ability to play it either way.

Determine the law firm's policy with respect to relay teams. This is a system in which a substitute is used if your original attorney becomes overcommitted or for other reasons—a personality conflict, perhaps—and concludes he cannot cross the finish line a winner for you. Ideally, you want a lawyer who will manage your case successfully from beginning to end. But the principal objective is to win and to do so without undue delay. The firm you select should share those objectives and have the capacity to fulfill them.

Don't be timid during your interviews. Be as aggressive as necessary in getting answers to your questions. You and your prospective counsel both need to know whether or not you can work together. And you want to know if, after a review of the basic facts, he is really enthusiastic about working on the case. Don't leave his office without finding out.

Since the majority of divorce lawyers are men, women should pay particular attention to their own reactions: are you more impressed by a lawyer's apparent competence and integrity or by his personal charm? Some divorce lawyers cultivate the role of Lothario. They are aware that some women, sitting in the ashes of a marriage that has gone up in flames, are under great stress. Because they may be questioning their own desirability as women, they may be highly susceptible to an opportunity to reassure themselves. Beware that touch of special interest, the dinner invitation that follows a late-afternoon appointment, or exaggerated compliments about your beauty and charm. They may simply be part of an attempt to exploit your susceptibility to masculine advances during an extremely trying time. If you yield to the temptation to mix business with pleasure, you may get the pleasure—but you're almost certain to "get the business," too.

Rule 6: Find Out What It's Going to Cost

Your initial interview, arranged to determine whether or not the lawyer will be retained, should cost you nothing. Beware the attorney who attempts to charge you for a preliminary conference or presses you for an immediate retainer to take your case. Don't, however, avoid the subject of fees. One of your most important objectives is to determine the probable fees for the legal services and court costs that will be involved.

Very likely, you will not have to introduce this subject yourself. Just as you are interested in learning the expenses involved, the lawyer will want to determine what the case is worth to him. His first questions will almost certainly seek to determine your assets and your income, and those of the other party involved.

When he asks these questions, be as unspecific as you can. Don't lie, but play it cool. Don't boast about your financial successes. Stall. Suffer a loss of memory about the precise extent of your assets. Be vague about your income. This information may determine the size of the attorney's fee. Whether you are the plaintiff or the defendant, it is to your advantage to minimize the legal fees: the more of the family's assets you can retain, the more there will be left with which each partner can begin a new life alone.

Playing down the extent of your income and assets at this point is crucial, because most lawyers will try to charge what they think you can afford. If you avoid giving the impression of affluence, it may reduce the amount of the retainer that is demanded, or it may result in a lower over-all cost, whether your financial arrangement is on an hourly basis or is a flat fee for the entire case.

Ultimately, of course, you will have to make more detailed financial disclosures to your lawyer and to the court. But if you have been adept at shielding your assets, and the costs for legal services have already been established, you will at least have gained a psychological advantage if not a real one. Your attorney won't have his mind set on making a killing on a single case. Nor, because he wants referral business, is he apt to risk the loss of your good will be raising his fees.

From the client's point of view, a flat, fixed fee is the ideal way to pay for a divorce. However, unless the case is so cut-and-dried the amount of effort involved is fully predictable, most good lawyers won't accept this arrangement. Unless you and your spouse have already agreed about the division of property and custody of the children and plan to settle out of court, don't expect to buy your decree with a tidy lump sum payment to the attorneys involved.

Many attorneys will quote a lump sum *estimate* to a prospective client, and some unscrupulous ones will underestimate the total cost in order to land a client. Don't be gullible and give your case to the lawyer who has quoted the lowest fee. You may find yourself in the position of the astronaut who asked what he was thinking as he sat in the space capsule waiting for blast-off. He replied that he was recalling the fact that the rocket had been assembled by those who made the lowest bids.

Repeatedly, disenchanted divorce clients have recounted to me their experiences with attorneys who, during the initial interview, assured them the case would cost only $1,000, or $1,500 at most. After the first court appearance, with the client safely hooked, the lawyer changed his tune. The case is a difficult one, goes the new song. It will take longer than he thought; it could even go on indefinitely. He will have to have an additional $500 or $1,000 if he is to stay on the case.

This technique is an obvious attempt to shake down the client and extract the highest possible fee. After low-balling the client to get his business, the attorney then progressively raises the price. The client, meanwhile, is in an almost untenable position. If he refuses to pay the additional sum and his lawyer drops the case, he loses the fees he has already paid and must begin anew with another attorney. If he agrees to the added fee, what is to prevent the lawyer from stalling the case through needless delays and continuances so he can again demand more money?

If an attorney offers to take your case for a specified flat fee, ask for his agreement in writing. And remember that an agreement to "handle your case" simply means the attorney agrees to take your case and represent you in court. It does not define the effort he will expend, the procedures he will employ, or the success he will achieve. Make sure your agreement spells out in detail the nature and extent of the services covered by the flat fee.

Many attorneys attempt to establish fees based on a percentage of the couple's total assets. This may be a reasonable approach, if the percentage is not too high or the assets too great. Often the attorney will seek an agreement that will give him 10 percent of the assets. This is probably unreasonable, unless it is a very small estate.

You will discover that rates charged in divorce cases often exceed those charged by the same attorneys of their permanent clients, simply because divorce tends to be a one-shot business and they may never see you again. In any event, before agreeing to a percentage arrangement, seek advice and exercise judgment, based on the experience of others, as to whether the percentage demanded appears to constitute a reasonable fee.

Don't, under any circumstances, permit your attorney to charge a contingency fee based on what he is able to collect in the form of alimony, support payments, or the division of assets. If such an arrangement is proposed, leave his office in haste, for you have identified another of the "dirty dozen." This practice is not only immoral, it is unethical and illegal as well.

In most instances, attorney's fees are determined by an hourly rate. You pay the lawyer as though you were hiring an electrician or a plumber—for the time he actually works. Even with this kind of arrangement, though, obtain a written agreement in advance that details the hourly rate and the activities for which you will be charged. Also stipulate that you will get more than a by-guess-and-by-golly accounting of the time the lawyer spends on your case. Stipulate that you will receive copies of the time sheets accounting for the effort spent in your behalf.

If you do agree to an hourly arrangement, be aware of the hidden costs that are involved. You are not paying simply for time in court. Phone conversations will appear on your lawyer's time sheet, and even a short conversation may appear as a quarter hour, which is often the minimum time recorded. If you are a victim of "telephonitis," don't let this habit persist when you are talking to your attorney, when an hour of his time may cost you fifty or seventy-five bucks. Unless it is an emergency, it is far cheaper to write a short note than to see your lawyer personally or even call him on the phone.

Your lawyer will probably be sufficiently adept at running up charges; he doesn't need any additional help from you. If you must talk to him, jot down the immediate problem before you call. Then stick to the point of discussion and resolve the problem as quickly as possible. Unless you can afford an expensive shoulder to cry on, cry on your mother's or that of a good friend. You are hiring a lawyer for legal services, not psychological counseling or emotional support. But the rates will be the same, whichever you get. All an attorney has to sell is his time and his advice. If you use his time to shoot the bull on other topics, whether in his office or on the phone, he will charge you for it. He has to, or he'd starve.

Find out if the lawyer charges additional fees for research, court time, office time and telephone conferences with others than yourself. Do office visits command a higher fee scale than telephone calls? If you ask his secretary for information, instead of talking directly to the lawyer, will you also be charged? You shouldn't be. Will you be charged the full $1.55 a page for the court reporter's transcripts if your lawyer is sharing them with the opposing attorney? You shouldn't be.

If you are determined to fight to hold your divorce costs to a minimum, you won't be timid about forcing your prospective attorney to be specific about his charges. If you fail to do so, and also to monitor costs closely throughout your case, you may be in for some unpleasant and costly surprises like the one this man recounted to me.

I wanted a witness to the fact that I was making my temporary alimony payments to my wife faithfully and on time, so I sent the check to my lawyer's office for forwarding to her. I felt a bit abused when I found he was charging me $37 for each check he processed.

I thought that was highway robbery, so I stopped sending the check to her through my lawyer and instead sent it directly to her lawyer. I figured that, if the lawyers charged $37 just to forward a check, I'd rather have her lawyer collect it from her than my lawyer collect it from me!

You should also investigate the attorney's reputation for diligence in the pursuit of a case. The opportunities for an attorney to multiply the hours spent in your behalf are almost limitless. Try to find one who will be as expeditious and as frugal of his time and your money as is possible.

Recently I had a revealing conversation with a woman who had retired after twenty years as a secretary in a divorce law firm. I asked her to tell me, on the basis of her experience, what she had learned. Here is her response, in her own words.

First of all, let's just say that I think lawyers drag out divorce cases. It doesn't really have to take that much time, and there doesn't need to be so much correspondence. Much of their activity is carried on so they can line their own pockets, and everything could really be much more simple.

Q. How do they drag it out?

A. Well, if a client asks a question, the lawyer will say, "We'll have to write the other attorney and wait for his answer to see what he says." Or he'd have me place a phone call and then report back to the client that he had talked to the opposing attorney and would have to wait for him to talk to his client. This sort of thing could go on and on, with the client paying for all of the letters and all of the telephone calls.

Sometimes clients would call me and say, "Don't ask your boss, because I just got a big bill for a few phone calls and can't afford any more, but can you tell me what's been going on since I was last in there?" Of course, I wasn't allowed to tell them anything, because the lawyer was in business to make money, not to give out information for free.

Q. What can the client do to make sure he gets a lawyer who will give him a fair shake?

A. There's not much he can do except talk to friends who have used divorce attorneys and find out if they thought the charges were fair. About the only thing you have to go on in picking a lawyer is his reputation. Some attorneys rip you off and others are reasonable. You just have to try to sort them out.

Q. Among the attorneys you know, do you feel that most of them charged fees that were reasonable?

A. No. I think most of them charged what they thought the traffic would bear.

Now, her experience may by no means be typical. Yet, it does give a clue as to what you could be up against. If you are not tough-minded about fees from the very beginning, you may find yourself in court twice—once for the divorce and again to appeal to the judge about your final bill. The latter may be a futile exercise. Remember that the judge was once a practicing lawyer, too.

Husbands, in considering the cost of a divorce, will do well to remember that historically they will be responsible for the fees charged by their attorney—and those of their spouse, as well. This practice arose because the husband usually had control of most of the assets and income and, to equalize the quality of representation, was also required to assume his wife's legal fees.

For a time, as the result of one Illinois case, it appeared that this traditional approach was being modified, and that the husband was relieved of responsibility for his wife's legal fees if her income exceeded his, or if she had substantial assets of her own. However, more recent cases have required the husband to assume the burden of his wife's legal fees even though both her income and assets were in excess of his.

If you are a man, your best bet is to assume you will be paying two lawyers, not one. Lawyers and judges are apt to follow the rule that "them that have, pay"—and a wife's income and assets rarely exceed those of her husband. However, neither husbands nor wives should submit readily to the exorbitant demands of greedy attorneys. If you are a woman, don't acquiesce to the kind of extortion experienced by one Illinois resident whose husband refused to pay her attorney's fees. Her attorney persuaded her to agree to pay them herself, promising to squeeze every last dime out of her husband in the final settlement. He kept his promise and got $10,000 from the husband—but he kept $9,000 for himself in legal fees and gave the distraught woman only $1,000.

A husband saddled with a double legal bill should also guard against unreasonable charges by his wife's attorney. If you have followed my advice, you will have a written agreement regarding fees with your own attorney, but you have no such agreement with the attorney who represented your wife. When you are presented with his bill, demand a detailed accounting of the time and expense it represents. If lawyers will take advantage of their own clients, you may be sure they will have even less compunction about defrauding a husband who was represented by somebody else.

I know one tenacious person whose wife's attorney presented him with an outrageous bill. He offered to settle for a figure he regarded as reasonable, about one-third the requested amount. When his offer was refused, he took the wife's lawyer to court and demanded an accurate record of the time he had spent on the case. He won a substantial reduction from an understanding judge.

Be tough! Negotiate if you think the legal fees are exorbitant. Often, the simple threat of taking the matter to court will win a reduction in the fee. Many lawyers would rather compromise than face the prospect of going before a judge to defend a clearly exorbitant fee and risking adverse publicity or word-of-mouth criticism of his charges.

Rule 7: Separate Counsel

No man, even a lawyer, can effectively serve two masters. Even though your decision to dissolve your marriage may be an amicable one, the divorce procedure remains an adversary system of justice. No one lawyer, even an old and trusted family friend, can equally counsel both partners. The false economy of engaging one attorney to represent both parties in a suit is a tempting one, but don't do it. If you do, you and your spouse will probably live to regret it. So may the lawyer, if he was a friend.

4

Pre-Court Strategy

You have exercised all of the care and caution recommended in the previous chapter and, from your master list of prospective attorneys, have selected the one who impressed you most. Until this moment, as you interrogated, evaluated, and investigated that lawyer, you have been adversaries. From this moment on you are allies.

If you and your attorney have concluded that reconciliation is neither possible nor desirable, you will begin to plan the strategy for what may well be the most important and trying contest of your life. This is a crucial period, because most divorces are decided long before they get to court.

You and your lawyer must contrive a game plan designed to win the most favorable settlement possible, whether it will be out of court or when your case goes to trial. Work closely and cooperatively with him or her; assist in every way you can. By helping your lawyer build a stronger case, you will enhance your chances of victory, save his time and thus reduce your legal fees.

Tactics: To Sue or Not to Sue?

If the option is open to you, one of your first decisions will involve your choice of role in the divorce action. Do you want to be the plaintiff or the defendant? Many lawyers—both divorce specialists and trial attorneys—will agree that, in most cases, it doesn't make much difference. Some, however—usually those who are most aggressive in the prosecution of a case—like to put their opponents on the defensive and prefer to represent the plaintiff. Others will decide that you should choose to be the defendant, forcing your spouse to prove his or her charges. Then you need only to refute successfully the charges and allegations made against you in order to win the case. Obviously, this choice is not open if your spouse does not want a divorce and refuses to bring suit.

The first to file and serve notice in the initial suit is regarded as the plaintiff. Whoever is served notice first is the defendant. The maneuvering involved provides the first battleground for the legal strategists.

A husband—or a wife—about to be served notice may wish to flee to a safe haven out of reach of the process server until he or she and the attorney have had an opportunity to decide if he or she wishes to be plaintiff or defendant. Once served notice, by registered mail or personally, it is too late.

How does a person know he is about to be served? Perhaps one spouse, in an angry and injudicious moment, tells the other she or he has hired a lawyer and wants a divorce. Or a warning may come, inadvertently or otherwise, from a mutual friend. In my own case, my wife's lawyer offered to serve notice on me at his office. My attorney and I decided we weren't going to make it any easier for them and refused the offer.

Spouses who have lost the skirmish over notice and missed the opportunity to be the plaintiff have other options open to them. If the case against them is weak and they have a stronger case of their own, they may crossfile—pressing their own grounds for divorce and petitioning for child custody. On the other hand, if the case against them is strong and defeat seems inevitable, they may simply not contest the charges. In that event, the spouse may be granted a divorce by default without having to prove anything.

If you choose this option you will, of course, risk losing

powerful bargaining points on questions of alimony and child custody, but you won't do it unless the assumption is that you probably would have lost them anyway. Meanwhile, default offers a quick and painless way of severing your marital ties. It also saves the expense of a long, costly, losing battle.

The best of circumstances, of course, is one in which cooperative partners resolved all questions out of court so that nothing remains but the granting of a divorce and court approval of pre-agreed settlement terms.

Finally, the legality of a new course of action called "divisible divorce" is now being tested in the Illinois courts. It is a procedure that could serve as a model for divorce reform measures throughout the country. Divisible divorce allows both partners, if they have a mutual desire to end the marriage and each has grounds, to divorce each other. Each partner, separately, gets a divorce from the other. It is a superb face-saving technique to salve the egos of mates who feel equally guilty—or guiltless—over the failure of their marriage.

Working With Your Lawyer

Your lawyer is your champion in and out of court. He or she is the knight who represents you in battle. But your relationship may be far more complex than that between, say, Lancelot and King Arthur.

Your healthily skeptical attitude toward him prior to his selection probably did little to assure him of your confidence. Now is the time to convince him you trust him and to develop a feeling of rapport. Persuade him you are behind him completely and want to cooperate fully with his efforts in your behalf. He'll work more effectively in an atmosphere of mutual trust.

Never, never lie to your lawyer or withhold information he may need. No client is more despised by an attorney than one who makes him look like a fool before a judge in a crowded courtroom. It is not unusual for a client to deceive his own champion, only to have his own attorney—and his case—shot down by the opposition. If, for example, you have lied to your attorney about your assets, and the facts are suddenly revealed in court by the opposition, your attorney will be embarrassed and your case probably lost. Once you have chosen your champion, level with him—or her—at all times.

Meanwhile, remain wary. Steal a glance over your shoulder now and then. The only real winners in a divorce action are lawyers, who collect the juicy fees. Prudence demands that you never *completely* trust even your own attorney because all of your interests are not identical. But you do want him to believe you do.

Inform yourself about the divorce laws and procedures in your state. Impress your attorney with your knowledge of his business. Be subtle about it, but make him prove to you along the way that he isn't letting you down. If you succeed at this, he'll be less tempted to shirk his responsibilities or sell you out.

How can you do this without being obvious or offensive? Be curious. Ask intelligent questions. Lawyers habitually obfuscate what is going on in court, particularly when they are dealing with female clients. The less their clients and the lay public know about the legal aspects of divorce, the less chance they will be asked to justify their actions. Beware of the lawyer who continually makes the process seem as complicated as possible. He may be fattening his fees by dragging out the proceedings.

Be suspicious if your lawyer does not promptly relay to you the messages conveyed by your spouse during the settlement proceedings. Lawyers have delayed cases for months simply by failing to convey information to their client or his mate. Why? Delays mean dollars to the attorneys involved.

Be watchful. Ask your lawyer to explain his actions. But don't be impetuous, and don't leap to hasty conclusions. Sometimes an attorney will not answer the opposing counsel's charges or allegations within the period required. He may, instead, request continuances and postponements. There often are legitimate reasons for this, but you should press for the reasons. Your attorney may want time to ascertain your opponents' strategy. He may be trying to catch them off guard. He may believe the psychological impact of delay may cause your spouse to accept a more reasonable settlement.

Don't be overly sensitive about your lawyer's personal attitude toward you, or even about the feelings he may convey about you to others. One man I know kept his lawyer even after learning, through cocktail party gossip, that his counsel had referred to him as a "whiny, crybaby complainer." The lawyer was a good one in his field, and to have changed lawyers would have resulted in delays and added costs. My friend swallowed his pride, kept his lawyer, and won his case.

Remember, you don't have to like your lawyer any more than he has to like or admire you. Yours is not a social relationship. When you engaged him, you weren't looking for a tennis partner or fishing companion. You wanted someone who could represent you effectively in court. If you have a tough case, there may be tense moments when your lawyer is less civil to you than you would like. Expect them, and don't be disturbed. Control your emotions and never, never say anything malicious about him.

There have been many cases in which clients who have made obscene and derogatory public comments about their attorneys later regretted it. Be forewarned that a lawyer can sue a client for defamation of character and win the case. Derogatory comments about a lawyer's legal ability may entitle him to sue and collect. Even though you believe, at the moment, that your attorney isn't representing you adequately, don't call him a "lousy lawyer." If you can't restrain yourself, at least qualify such statements with "I think," "I believe" or "in my opinion." Better still, bite your tongue, count to ten and keep your opinions to yourself. You're a cinch to get more help from a friend than an enemy, and you may avoid a costly suit, besides.

Sessions With Your Lawyer

Your lawyer, if he is a good one, will charge between fifty and seventy-five dollars an hour and, if you are wealthy, may charge even more. When you meet with him, don't waste his time and your money.

Come to each conference armed with a concise set of notes covering what you want to discuss and get to the point quickly. The clock is ticking, whether you are giving him important information about your case, which is essential, or regaling him with your favorite bartender's latest joke, which is not.

Gather as much of the background material your lawyer will need as you possibly can: if he has to do it for you, it will cost you money. But don't burden him with extraneous detail or petulant opinions about your mate. Stick to the point. Don't ramble. Find out what you need to know, but don't ask needless questions. And don't, for heaven's sake, treat a legal conference as a social hour. There are less expensive forms of entertainment.

What to Tell Your Attorney About Your Assets

Divorce is really about money: alimony for the wife, support for the children, fees for the attorneys and, if he plays his cards right and is willing to fight, economic survival for the husband. If you have skillfully applied the advice offered in Chapter 2, you should already have protected a significant portion of your assets. But the struggle isn't over. Complete and detailed information on your financial condition is something every lawyer involved will try to obtain.

Your job as a client, if you are the breadwinner, is to convince your attorney that your assets and earnings are diminished so you can retain as many resources as possible after the divorce.

In discussing finances with your attorney, for example, you might imply that, because of the mental harassment, restrictions on visits with your children and other actions of your mate, your psychological condition has deteriorated and your income is down. This is a plausible condition because it often is true. The husbands I interviewed repeatedly described the deterioration of their businesses and the sale of assets in order to survive.

You should anticipate, where income and assets are concerned, that your own lawyer will subject you to the third degree. You will probably be asked to supply copies of your tax returns and lists of your assets. Your attorney may even call your employer to verify your salary, or your competitors to check on sales volume. If you are too evasive, he may accuse you of lacking confidence in him and threaten to resign from the case.

Hang in there. At this early stage in the proceedings, if your lawyer is too demanding, perhaps you made a mistake. Your interests might be better served if he did resign. Many a husband has emerged from court penniless because he was too open with his own lawyer about the extent and nature of his assets. Remember, your attorney will confer with your spouse's attorney on the issue of your assets and income. Nothing you tell him, even confidentially, will be kept from your opponent's attorney. Use every legal ruse you can to minimize your assets because, if you don't look after yourself on this issue, you can be sure no one else will.

You don't have to lie to your lawyer, nor am I suggesting that you do. In fact, should you deliberately falsify, conceal or secrete assets from the court, the judge will be rough on you. If you don't provide substantially accurate information in response to specific questions, your failure to do so is grounds for voiding the settlement.

But do you need to *volunteer* every last bit of information about your financial condition? I don't think so. Let's say you have reinvested some of your securities and made a killing. Do you need to tell anyone, unless you are asked a specific question? Why not say your assets are substantially unchanged and let it go at that? As of that precise moment, they *are* unchanged.

Much of this gets to be a matter of semantics. Avoid positive words like *exactly, every, always* and *never*. Instead, use words like *about, approximately, substantially, I believe,* and *I think*. You never quite lie, yet you try to avoid revealing to your attorney, and to his opponent, the full extent of your income and assets. You simply strive to convey the impression that you are less affluent than both lawyers had hoped you would be.

Without resorting to outright deception, present the least rosy impression of your assets and income that you can. Then, in response to the further inquiries that are certain to be made as time goes by, continue the charade. Your business has declined. Your debts and obligations have increased. Use every device you can to convey the impression you are gradually being impoverished. But do so without actually lying to your attorney. You want to negotiate the lowest settlement possible and also to hold down those legal fees. After the divorce, should you wish to confer assets on your ex-mate or children, that's your privilege. At least it will be your choice.

Meanwhile, reversing the situation, try to obtain all the financial information you can about your spouse. Know the trends in his or her business. Try to determine if he or she is faking financial disclosures, arranging with employers to postpone bonuses or otherwise minimizing earnings or secreting assets in the names of others. Husbands have been known to transfer assets to the names of parents, siblings, even girlfriends. Others have quietly moved a portion of their business outside their own state's jurisdiction, or even out of the country, to make it appear that their local business is declining.

This is the case with a suburban Chicago man whose wife and a succession of lawyers have spent literally years trying to pin down the value of the assets he has acquired through inheritance and in the operation of his own business. The husband, forewarned he might be sued for divorce, transferred all of his assets to Swiss bank accounts, other than property held jointly in the U.S. with his wife. She and her lawyers have yet to prove to the court that the foreign assets actually exist, and she has been granted only her share of the real property jointly held with her husband in the U.S.

Keeping Records and Safeguarding Documents

If you anticipate a complex, drawn out court case and don't own a filing cabinet, go out and buy one. You're out to win this battle. To do that, you're going to acquire mountains of paper, documents and notes. If you're wise, you will become a legal pack rat.

On what aspects of your case should you keep records? Virtually all of them. Keep complete and accurate records of your meetings and telephone conversations with your attorney.

Note the date and the time that elapsed. Include information on the purpose of the conversation, who instigated it and the subjects covered. You may need this information for tax purposes or to verify the accuracy of your attorney's bill or even to use in court, if you dispute his charges.

Avoid giving your attorney original copies of personal documents and records that are important to your case. Make photocopies and let him work with those unless and until it may be necessary to present the originals in court. Why this caution? Because some attorneys, as they rush from one courtroom to another, become careless and leave important papers behind. The divorcees I interviewed repeatedly recounted incidents of this kind. One lost some valuable evidence when her attorney placed the envelope containing it on a courtroom table while conferring with opposing council. When they finished talking, the envelope was gone.

In addition to the possibility that valuable documents may be lost or stolen, there is also the chance a harried secretary in a busy office may place them in the wrong file or, should you decide to change attorneys, that they will deliberately be withheld from you. One of my friends was compelled to go through a costly court action to retrieve his case file from a lawyer he had fired. Another retrieved his documents only after writing a letter of complaint to the Judicial Law Review.

One woman, whose husband was trying to misrepresent the magnitude of his income, developed a "fantastic presentation" to demonstrate the devious ways in which he had cheated on his income tax returns. Then she changed lawyers.

"The lawyers had many of my personal documents in the trunks of their cars," she recalls. "I was horrified when they told me where they were. There were so many important documents, including evidence to prove that my husband had stolen from me. I finally recovered some of my papers, but the rest are still in their possession and they will not give them up.

"Actually, I don't think they can find all of my things in their office because it is such a mess all the time. There are still many documents missing from my file."

When I asked her why she hadn't retained duplicate copies of her records, she replied that it would have cost a small fortune. She had not considered that the cost would have been minimal compared to the fortune she lost by failing to do so.

Unless you have retained possession of important documents, you may sustain a lengthy delay if you decide to change attorneys. Many lawyers will refuse to surrender your file to a new lawyer until they have been paid. They are entitled to their legitimate fees, of course, but if you are being overcharged and are compelled to dispute the fees, you will be unable to retrieve the documents that are vital to your case. Lacking records your new lawyer requires will delay your case.

Good records may also be important in determining whether you or your spouse will be granted custody of the children. Here's some sound advice from one of my friends, based on her own experience.

> I think it's important, particularly when there are children involved and there are any problems at all, to keep correspondence and the envelopes and to make photocopies of the correspondence as well as the envelopes, in case they are lost, borrowed or stolen. I think it's also important, if you're having a lot of problems, to take notes on phone calls—the date, time, and essence of what was said during these conversations.
>
> Secondly, if you're not the visiting parent, it's important to take notes on when that parent comes, the length of the stay, what attitudes were displayed by the child and the visiting parent, even how the other parent was dressed. Note whether the child and visiting parent returned on time and if the child was upset.
>
> All these things may be important. Write down everything pertinent that your child says. Don't trust your memory. If you have to give testimony on these things, it will be much more credible if you can sustain your testimony with careful notes rather than a vague reply, like "I think it was a couple of months ago."
>
> Fortunately, I did all of these things instinctively because I was terribly upset at the time and didn't trust my memory. Later I was glad I had been so careful.
>
> Even if your notes prove to have no legal value, I think they do something else for you. When you feel an emotion and know why you feel that way, write it down. It may be something your former husband or wife has said, or something your child has done, that

> you feel a certain way about. Write it down. It will help you analyze and deal with that problem later, if not right then.
>
> I also think, if you have children and there is a custody battle or fight over visitation rights, it is very important—at least it was in my case—to write a description of your child as if you were going to tell a total stranger everything possible about the child so the stranger would be able to get to know him. To take care of him, let's say, while you were going to be away. Everything from a description of the child's personality to what he likes to eat or play with.
>
> Doing this will not only help your lawyer, it will also help you: when you get on the witness stand, you will be able to think more clearly. Until you have been on the witness stand you don't know how nervous you can be or how things you should know instinctively you simply can't remember. People have even forgotten their own names, they've been so nervous. So it's important to have everything overlearned and oversimplified, especially if you've never been a witness before.

Everything she says I've heard from many others.

Court records are also important and should be retained indefinitely after your case has been decided, in the event there is post-decree litigation. Courts retain records for about seven years, but your need for them may continue over a longer period. Let's assume, for example, that your custodial ex-wife is killed in an auto accident many years after the divorce. You could become involved in child custody litigation with your in-laws, and the records and evidence used in your divorce action could be essential in proving your fitness as a parent.

What If Your Attorney Resigns?

Should your counsel resign, it's not the end of the world. What is more important is the manner in which he resigns. Don't let him take any actions that may prejudice your case in the future.

A lawyers may decide to resign for many reasons. Sometimes he may feel there has been a breach of confidence between him and his client. In other cases, he may find he doesn't have time to handle what has become an unusually complicated case, or that he is not qualified to cope with a case involving intricate financial aspects.

One of my friends retained a lawyer who was a member of a large metropolitan law firm. A few days later, she was called to his office and told he was resigning from the case because he was too busy. As she was leaving, she glanced at some of the papers on his desk. One of them concerned a legal action in which his firm was representing a large corporation of which her husband was an officer. She then realized the law firm had decided it couldn't risk losing the corporation's business by representing her.

Obviously, in one of these situations, it would be pointless to fret over losing the lawyer because, in the circumstances described, you wouldn't want him on your side, anyway.

You may spot a potential resignation in the offing if your attorney tries the co-counsel ploy. He may suggest you hire a co-counsel who specializes in your type of divorce case. Then, a few weeks later—offering a good excuse—he resigns. His conscience will be reasonably clear because he can say, "After all, you still have Mr. Co-Counsel, who is a fine attorney."

If your attorney resigns for any reason, don't pass up the opportunity to negotiate a lowered fee. He should not be paid as much as if he had directed the case to a successful conclusion. If you fire your attorney, however, you will probably have to pay his full fee. If you are a fighter, this leads to an obvious strategic conclusion: if you want to get rid of your lawyer, try to provoke his resignation. If he resigns, he may feel obliged to accept a reduced fee, accept what you have already paid him or give you a partial refund.

Don't Be Afraid to Change Attorneys

It is less apt to happen if you have selected your attorney carefully, but the time may come when you should consider resigning as your attorney's client. The following may be good reasons for doing so.

1. He is guilty of interminable and needless delays.
2. He does not seem to have your best interests at heart.
3. He is uncommunicative and inaccessible.
4. He is not following your instructions in representing you in court.

5. He seems to be taking you for a financial ride.
6. He seems too busy to devote an adequate amount of time to you and your case.
7. You suspect collusion with opposing counsel and really do not trust him.

How you go about changing attorneys is very important. Usually, no self-respecting replacement will talk to you until you are a "free agent." You must get permission from your present counsel before you can even approach another lawyer. Otherwise, you might upset some of the plans he has made for your case.

One way of determining the availability of other counsel without putting your present attorney on notice is to have a trusted friend or relative do some spade work. Without mentioning your name, he or she can make inquiries to locate a good replacement with the time and inclination to take the case.

Once you have found a new attorney, be prepared to pay your original lawyer at once. Until you do, he will be unwilling to turn your file over to another counsel.

But before you do anything, be sure you really want to make a change. Is your dissatisfaction only the result of a misunderstanding? Are you simply impatient? Have you failed to recognize the purpose of some of your lawyer's actions and the need for some of the delays? Could your doubts be cleared up by a frank, nondefensive discussion with him? Most important, can you afford the added expense and the additional delay?

What's Involved in Suing Your Lawyer

A surgeon who leaves a forceps in a patient can kill him. A lawyer who commits a careless or malicious legal error can kill your case in court. As in the case of physicians and surgeons, the law makes it possible for you to seek retribution and compensation for legal mistakes as well as medical ones. In recent years, malpractice suits against attorneys have been on the increase. The only difference between medical and legal malpractice is that doctors often bury their mistakes. The victim of legal malpractice has to live with them.

Winning a suit for legal malpractice is not easy, however. Cadwalader Menk, former president of the Chicago Bar Association, says the most common cause for malpractice suits against lawyers is their failure to meet certain deadlines, resulting in losses for the client.

"In cases like this, the malpractice issue is usually pretty clear," Menk says. "Either the lawyer did or did not meet the deadlines. But proving a lawyer was guilty of malpractice because he didn't handle the case in the best way is much more difficult because that essentially involves value judgments."

When might a divorce client want to sue his counsel?

One dentist did because his attorney failed to notify him of a court appearance. Because he failed to appear in court, his case was lost by default. Frequently, suing your attorney may be the only recourse in seeking reduction of an exorbitant fee. An unfair settlement stemming from collusion with opposing counsel might offer another reason.

In July, 1976, a Chicago man, Stanley Robel, won an $80,000 award in Cook County Circuit Court because his lawyer failed to appear in court in his behalf and his wife was awarded a house, the furniture and forty acres of land. He sued the attorney, Thomas Rudnick, for failing to properly represent him, with the result that his property was lost by default.

The jury agreed that Rudnick was guilty of legal malpractice and ruled in favor of Robel. The attorney, Harvey Sussman, who undertook the suit against Rudnick, said he had mixed feelings about the size of the award but believes that lawyers, like doctors, should police malpractice among their colleagues.

"We have an obligation to clean up the legal profession," Sussman said.

Sussman's attitude is more constructive than that of some in his profession. Victims of legal malpractice have often found it difficult to find a lawyer willing to sue another member of the bar association. The profession is a sort of tightly-knit club when the general interests of lawyers are threatened, and the example of increasing medical malpractice suits has made it even more difficult to find one lawyer willing to blow the whistle on another. The reasoning is this: if such cases get publicity, it may plant seeds in the minds of other victims. In other cases, victims of malpractice may simply be in a position where they can't afford to sue. When their attorney got through with them, they were broke.

In any event, there is one more recourse against unscrupulous attorneys who prey on emotionally upset divorce clients. This is the local bar association. If enough complaints are lodged against an unscrupulous lawyer, he may be investigated and perhaps disbarred.

But even if your complaint to the bar association does not produce so drastic a result, it may, in situations where you are being overcharged, secure a reduction in the fee. One Illinois woman retained an attorney to assist her in obtaining an increase in child support payments. He told her there would be a nominal fee of $50 to cover the cost of recording the papers and filing the suit and that the additional fees would be assessed against her ex-husband. However, on completing the case, he submitted a bill for $375.

"I had to pursue the issue by going to the bar association," she says, "and talk to the president of the bar association to have him straighten things out for me. He was very friendly and helpful. He talked to my attorney and convinced him I shouldn't be charged the total fee. My attorney then charged my ex-husband $75 and me $100, for a total of $175. I still felt that was unfair, but I did save $200."

5

The Walls May Have Ears

ALL of the bromides associated with military science apply to divorce, as well. "All's fair in love and war." "The best defense is a good offense." "War is hell."

And the parallels aren't really surprising, because divorce, like warfare, is the final resort employed by two parties when long-standing disputes can't be resolved by any other means.

This chapter is a martial arts course for those on the eve of marital warfare. It will be particularly useful to those with limited financial resources who are willing to do for themselves some of the work that a lawyer or private detective would otherwise be paid to do.

The Need for Information

These may be days of tension, confusion and uncertainty. Perhaps your spouse has stormed angrily out of the house after announcing his or her intentions to file for a divorce. Then, silence. You bite your nails, drink too many martinis and wonder why you haven't been served notice. Why doesn't something happen? What's the delay?

Preserve your fingernails and skip the martinis. More than

ever before in your life, you need to reason calmly and think clearly. Start applying what you have already learned here and watch yourself. There may be a sinister reason for the delay.

In many cases, lawyers do not file suit immediately because they hope, through surveillance of the other spouse, to develop additional grounds that will strengthen their client's complaint. A lawyer may have few provable charges against you and hope you will drop your guard and give him the proof he needs to win in court.

Sometimes an attorney will wait six months or longer before filing on grounds alleged by your spouse during your last bitter argument. If he is unable to develop new evidence, he files on the basis of the information he had at the outset. If you are indiscreet and enable him to develop new information during the waiting period, he will have a stronger case. Sometimes a complaint may be amended to add new charges developed out of investigation that strengthen the original grounds.

If you are up against one of the "dirty dozen," he and your spouse may be plotting a malicious or demeaning campaign against you. They may try to manufacture evidence of adultery, homosexuality, lesbianism, drug abuse or alcoholism that will help them win their case.

They may even be recruiting witnesses who are willing to commit perjury to strengthen their case. Sound unlikely? One of my friends plays tennis with a woman who formerly worked as a secretary for a firm of divorce lawyers. One of her duties, when asked, was to appear as a witness to allegations made by plaintiff clients. If, for example, one of the grounds for divorce was an allegation that the husband had beaten his wife, she would appear in court to testify that she had witnessed the beating.

It is some measure of human avarice that she rationalized her perjury with the assertion that she had no reason to disbelieve the client. She could accept the fact that, for her perjured testimony, she received extra compensation.

Immoral and illegal activities of this kind are far from routine. Odds are they won't happen to you, but they have happened to many others and *could* happen to you. So why accept the normal odds? Your best bet is to improve them in your favor. Watch your behavior during this critical period. Be careful what you do and say. Carefully plan your own defense and offense, and be alert to the offense your spouse and the opposing attorney may be planning against you.

Learn About Your Spouse's Counsel

If you have followed our advice and gone through the tedious and essential process of researching your own choice of an attorney, you will already have identified many of the "dirty dozen." Is your spouse's counsel one of them? If not, and if he or she was not one of those you have already investigated, you should begin your research anew and learn everything you can about him.

Ask every lawyer you know for an opinion of your spouse's attorney. Ask about his or her personal life and his educational background. Find out how articulate he is in the courtroom. Discover how honest he is. Ask about his courtroom tactics. Determine if he routinely uses private investigators to develop evidence for his clients. Learn to recognize his voice and, if possible, the voices of his partners, secretary, and wife. Be able to recognize those voices in case surreptitious phone calls are made to gain information about you.

Attempts to Investigate You

I don't want you to become paranoid about the ordeal you are facing, but you should be aware of several ruses that could be used in an attempt by your spouse and attorney to gain evidence against you. Again, they are not typical, but they happen often enough that you should be on guard against them. If you are aware of these techniques, you may avoid pitfalls along the well-worn path to divorce.

Although telephone wiretaps are illegal unless ordered by the court in highly restricted circumstances, and, although evidence obtained by illegal wiretaps is inadmissable in court, don't overlook the possibility that such a tap may be installed in your home or office. Even though the information gained cannot be used directly, it may enable a private investigator to more readily monitor your daily activities and alert your spouse to behavior that provides further grounds for divorce.

One alert husband, convinced his wife was guilty of adultery but unable to prove it, helped an investigator gather the evidence he needed by bugging his own home telephone. Here is his story.

> At the time of my problem, I put a bug on my phone at home. It was about the size of a matchbook and cost $150. Actually, the device was a wireless transmitter that could be picked up on an unused FM channel on my radio.
>
> I buried the transmitter in our basement ceiling. I had to take out a little piece of plaster, insert the bug, and then replaster it in. I hooked it up to the telephone lines with two small wires that weren't detectable. I had an FM radio in a remote part of the house attached to a voice-activated tape recorder that was tuned in on the frequency of the transmitting device. Every time the phone rang, the tape recorder was activated. When my wife hung up the phone, the recorder would stop.
>
> Through this device I was able to find out exactly when and where she was going to meet with anyone. It was then a simple matter to inform the detective so he could follow her. He got the evidence I needed without wasting a lot of time and running up his fees. It was all I needed to get my divorce and custody of my children as well.

Sophisticated devices of this kind are virtually impossible to detect. In fact, in the case cited, the wife suspected that the phone was being tapped; on several occasions she had the telephone company check the line, but they found nothing. If the client is willing and able to pay the costs, and the risks of making the installation are not too great, a private investigator also might install such a device. But simpler, more readily detectable taps are more common.

Contrary to a popular misconception, contemporary telephone taps don't make clicking noises. In fact, they do not even have to be attached directly to the telephone line. It is possible, simply by being near the line, to monitor the conversation. Nevertheless, you do have some defenses against the most common and least sophisticated taps. Gene Allen, president of E. V. Allen and Associates, Inc., a firm of private investigators in Chicago, offers the following advice.

> If you suspect a tap on your telephone, you should obtain another instrument from another location, put them side by side, and examine the components. You can take the case off very easily with a screwdriver, unthread the mouth and ear pieces, and compare components. If they don't match, your phone has probably been violated.
>
> The phone company will do a physical check for you and they will also do an impedance check on your line to see if there is a parasite attached. This is a resistance test that will reveal whether or not there is an extra load on your line; they can make it from the switching station without even coming to your house.

Your best bet, if you suspect a tap, is simply to be careful what you say over the telephone. If your call is one you don't want your spouse or a lawyer to hear, make it from a pay phone.

Remember, most wiretappers don't leave a tap on continuously. They tap occasionally. And you can be bugged by means other than your telephone. There may be a long-range eavesdropping device outside your home, or a miniatuie microphone fitted into a light fixture. James Bond didn't retire: he went to work for a divorce lawyer.

How to Tell If You're Being Tailed

In domestic relations cases, private detectives are often hired to follow a husband or wife to try to collect damaging evidence against him or her. If your conduct may generate such evidence, you have two choices. The safer one is simply to refrain from questionable behavior until the court has rendered its decision and you are free to do as you please. But if that is a higher price than you are willing to pay, at least be alert to the possibility that someone may be following you.

There is no sure way you can detect pursuit, but knowledge of the techniques investigators use may help. One obvious clue is a small hole punched in the red taillight cover of your car. This method is used to make it easier for the pursuer to identify the car being followed. The little hole will send out a beacon of white light and distinguish your vehicle from others on a dark highway.

If you find such a hole, let it be a "red light" warning to you. Change cars or have the red cover repaired or replaced.

Another obvious way to detect a bloodhound on your trail is to take a devious route, either on foot or in a car—one that no one would be apt to use to get from one place to another. Watch who follows you wherever you turn. If one individual or automobile remains behind you continuously over a long and circuitous route, you should assume that it isn't coincidental.

This precaution won't help you much, however, if you are being tailed by a sophisticated and well-paid investigative firm, because they won't rely on a single pursuer. They may use as many as three investigators with mobile radios who alternate in pursuit. While one is behind you, the others will be moving at the same pace on parallel streets and will switch places periodically. This makes pursuit almost impossible to detect and is another argument for irreproachable behavior while your case is in court. This is expensive surveillance, but if the stakes are high enough, your spouse may be willing to pay for it.

Finally, without seeing spooks behind every tree or isolating yourself like a hermit, be aware of strangers who visit or are seen frequently around your home. They may be observing who visits you or how carefully you supervise the children. Private investigators may pose as salesmen, repairmen, or even meter readers to gain access to your home in their search for information. Be careful. Don't make their job easy for them.

Investigation Works Both Ways

Just as you are vulnerable to investigation by your spouse, he or she is also vulnerable to yours. You, too, have the option of employing an investigator, if you can afford it, and you also have the opportunity to do your own investigating. While your case is in progress, put yourself on red alert. If your eyes and ears are at their battle stations, you may be surprised by what you learn.

For example, one wife got out her stationery pad one day to

write a note and accidentally flipped it open so the cardboard backing was exposed. She noticed some indentations in it and penciled over the marks to reveal a note addressed, "Dear Sue." It was signed, "Bob." Because her husband's name was Phil and she wasn't Sue, and there was no Bob or Sue in the house, she knew at once that something strange was going on. She then recalled several recent calls for "Bob" that she had dismissed as wrong numbers. Putting the two together, she launched an investigation that ended with an adultery charge against her husband.

Another wife intercepted an airline's call to her husband confirming an 8:30 flight to Acapulco for Mr. and Mrs. Her husband hadn't invited her to go to Acapulco with him, but she said nothing to him about the call. Instead she went to the airport with a witness who identified her husband and his sexy girlfriend in the passenger lounge.

She waited until the flight was called and then approached the pair as they were about to board the plane. Her husband was speechless and she so angry that, after a few appropriate comments, she vigorously demanded he give her five hundred dollars, then and there. Flustered and embarrassed, he pulled out his wallet, peeled off five one-hundred-dollar bills and departed for Mexico. The money came in handy as a down payment for her lawyer when she filed suit for divorce.

When she told the story on the witness stand, she won some extra sympathy from the judge by revealing that, when she traveled with her husband, they flew coach. He and his girlfriend had traveled first class!

Another suspicious wife couldn't pin anything on her husband until she borrowed his car one day. When she opened the glove compartment, searching for a street map, she found a package of contraceptives. Since she had been on the Pill for years, she was more than curious about their presence, but she said nothing. Instead, she began checking her husband's car periodically, after his late evenings at the office, and observed that the devices gradually disappeared. With some help from an investigator, that was the beginning of the end for their marriage.

In addition to the methods of eavesdropping already discussed, a suspicious spouse can monitor telephone calls legally and conveniently with the full cooperation of the telephone company. Suppose, for example, that a husband wants to eavesdrop on the calls his wife makes from his home phone during his work day at the office. The telephone company will cheerfully—even eagerly—install a home extension phone in your business office. They will also bill you for the service at your office. After it has been installed, remove the mouthpiece so your wife won't hear extraneous noises. You now have an alert and convenient spy poised at your elbow. If you wish, you can even have a duplicate extension installed at your office so a witness can listen, too.

It is also possible to enlist the aid of the telephone company to obtain a list of all outgoing calls made from any telephone. If you live in a large metropolitan area where local service charges are based on message units, you may call the bookkeeping office and request, for verification of charges, that they supply you with a list of the calls for which you are being billed. You will receive a detailed report that will include the telephone number called, the date and time the call was made and the number of units charged. On request, the telephone company will also place a device on your line that will list every number dialed for a two-week period.

One final word on do-it-yourself investigative work. Don't try to do your own surveillance. You may find you have enough basic information to indicate that surveillance of your spouse will provide the evidence you need to win your case. If so, act on your suspicions, but hire a trained investigator to do it; such evidence-gathering requires professional skill. Moreover, if you act as your own sleuth, the odds you will get caught and alert your spouse to your investigative efforts are far too great. Leave the job to an experienced stranger.

There are exceptions to every rule, of course. People have been known to employ incredibly ingenious devices to gather evidence against erring mates. One wife was convinced her husband was cheating but had no proof. One day she decided to follow him when he left, as usual, for work. He took a circuitous route and parked in the driveway of a neighbor woman who lived a relatively short distance away.

Although she saw him enter the house, his wife was now confronted with the problem of proving that his presence in the house was something more than a polite social call.

Suddenly inspired, she hurried back to her own home and called the fire department. She gave the address of the house her husband was visiting, reporting that it was on fire and she was locked in a bedroom at the rear of the house and couldn't get out. She asked that the firemen break down the front door and hurry to the bedroom to free her.

The wife then returned to the neighbor's house to watch. The firemen arrived almost immediately and quickly broke in the front door. As they hurried to the bedroom, the wife was right behind. When they opened the door, she had the bare facts she needed to get her divorce and plenty of witnesses. The firemen found no fire, but they saw a marriage go up in flames. The wife, incidentally, had the presence of mind to get their names and addresses, and when her divorce action went to trial she subpoenaed them as witnesses to her husband's infidelity.

Hiring a Private Detective

There may come a time, despite all of your own investigative efforts, when you or your attorney may decide you need the services of a private detective agency. Because of some of the stories you have read about detectives peeping through hotel room transoms, this may have a sordid connotation to you. It shouldn't. Many legitimate and necessary services are performed by investigators, and they are engaged by thousands of individuals and hundreds of business firms every year. Anyway, sordid or not, you are fighting for your future, no holds barred.

If your lawyer recommends that you employ an investigator, he probably will also suggest which firm you should engage. If you have developed absolute confidence in him, you probably should take his advice. If not, some investigation is in order before deciding which firm you want to use.

Many of the individuals I interviewed recounted bitter and costly experiences with incompetent investigators. One man who suspected his wife was a lesbian paid $1,500 in advance to an investigator to try to confirm that as fact. He supplied the detective with information and ten days later received an oral report that ten persons had been contacted who shared the husband's suspicions.

"I told him I could have conducted that kind of a survey," the husband recalls. "I paid for an investigation and got a public opinion poll. But I asked him at least to give me a written report for my money. He then became impossible to find. I called him periodically, always getting the brush from his secretary. Finally, two years ago, I met him on the street and extracted a promise from him that he would return half of the $1,500 I had paid him and give me a written report in return for the other half.

"Despite repeated attempts, I heard nothing further from or about him. I didn't get my $750 or the report. He finally surfaced again a few weeks ago, on the afternoon news on TV. He is going through bankruptcy and I have about as much chance of getting the report or seeing my $750 as I have of seeing the reincarnation!"

Another of my friends, who lives in Chicago, was told by his attorney that the services of a detective in Arizona would be required to prove a document submitted by his wife was a forgery. The attorney requested and was given a check for $1,000 to cover the detective's fee. Within a few weeks, a report was received from the investigator confirming that the document had been forged.

In this case, however, the villian of the piece was the attorney and not the detective. Later that year, my friend had occasion to visit Arizona and out of curiosity called on the owner of the detective agency.

"The president of the company was very cordial and willing to discuss with me what he did and when he did it. On a hunch, I then asked him how much he was paid for this work. He couldn't find the bill but went to his ledger and reported that he was paid $292 for his services. The balance of the $1,000 check that had been sent him had been returned to my attorney. In other words, the attorney put in his pocket $708 of my money that allegedly went for detective services."

Experiences such as this suggest that the selection of an investigative firm is not something you should go into blindly, even if the firm is recommended by your own attorney. It is not unusual for attorneys to engage a detective for a few dollars an hour, charge the client $25 and pocket the difference. Besides, in many states, it is easier to become a "private investigator" than it is to become a dog catcher. Fewer than half of the fifty states have requirements for the licensing of private detectives. All a person needs to become a detective is enough money to pay for an office and a sign for the door. And of those states that do have licensing procedures, only a few—perhaps seven—make any earnest effort to maintain strict standards and to enforce them for the protection of the individual client. As a result, there are countless agencies to choose from, but many of them are unprofessional, slipshod or just plain dishonest.

Knowing this, don't look for a detective agency the way you might shop for a toaster or a transistor radio. Use as much care as you would use in choosing a doctor, dentist, insurance agent, realtor—or a lawyer. Maybe more!

Listen again to Gene Allen, one of the real pros in the investigative field. He's had more than twenty years of investigative training and experience—as a special agent of the Federal Bureau of Investigation, later in business and recently as head of his own rapidly growing private agency.

He's a lawyer by training. And he's young enough, despite his years of experience, to be in touch with new technological developments and all of the modern investigative techniques.

"Our business has grown mainly through referrals," Allen says. "We do a good, solid job for our clients, and many of them tell their friends and business associates about us. And many of these people come to us for help. It's a matter of personal trust."

Mutual confidence and trust are undoubtedly the most important elements in the client-detective relationship. The integrity of the firm you select is also important because, if it operates illegally in your behalf, it may involve you in a conspiracy charge. Here are some guidelines to use in selecting a private agency.

Rule 1

Try to find someone in whom you have confidence who has recently hired a private detective agency. This person could be a good friend, a close business acquaintance, a respected banking contact or an insurance company investigator. Once you've found him, ask if the service provided was adequate—effective, prompt, reasonably priced, confidential. Ask if he'd hire the agency again. It possible, try to find an investigative firm that has worked on a case similar to yours. With luck, you'll be able to find one that gets a warm recommendation, based on a recent job they've done for someone whose judgment you respect.

Rule 2

Most reputable attorneys who specialize in domestic cases frequently use the services of investigative agencies. They may be willing to give you the names of three or four agencies or individuals who have served them well.

In addition, there is an organization called the Society of Former Agents of the Federal Bureau of Investigation; its headquarters are in New York City. Its executive secretary may be able to provide you with a list of investigative agencies in your city. Most major cities have private agencies staffed with former FBI men. They maintain close working relationships with their fellow alumni in other cities, giving you, in effect, a network of agencies that can be national in scope. FBI training and experience provide some assurance you are getting a well-trained, experienced private investigator.

If you're still unable to locate a qualified firm, turn to the Yellow Pages of your local telephone directory. But, as Gene Allen points out, a few words of caution are in order here.

Rule 3

Visit your local library and check back through the Yellow Pages for several years. Make sure the names you select have appeared every year, for many agencies are active for a year or so and then fold their tents, often leaving unpaid bills, unfinished cases and disappointed clients behind them. Make sure the services offered include "domestic" investigations. Note if the firm's address is in a high-rent district or suggests it may be a sleazy operation. You can also tell something about the agency from the size and effectiveness of its ad, but a big ad doesn't always mean a big firm, nor does a big firm always mean an honest, effective operation. A more reliable criterion, often noted in the ads, is how long the firm has been in business. If it's been around for half a century, it's probably pretty good.

All right, let's say you have located a prospective agency by one of these routes, preferably the first. There's a final, most important step to take.

Rule 4

Make an appointment to visit the office of the agency. Investigate the investigator.

Is the office neat and orderly? Is it in a business neighborhood? (Some private investigators operate out of their homes and have few supporting resources to call on if a case requires them.) Is the agency and its staff duly licensed under the applicable state and local laws? Have its people had substantial experience in many investigative cases, preferably with some background in law enforcement work?

Remember that, although you engage the firm, your case will be assigned to an individual and you have no guarantee his skills and experience equal the firm's reputation. So ask about the qualifications of the investigator who will be assigned to your case; meet him if possible. Note his personal appearance and manner, for he may have to be a reliable, unimpeachable witness in court. Ask the agency for references and don't fail to check them out before you proceed. Determine whether or not he has filed a performance bond with the appropriate agency against which you can proceed in the event of fraud.

Then go into fees. Most agencies charge on an hourly basis, and—particularly if surveillance is involved—the hours can mount at an incredible rate. Gene Allen recommends that you establish a flat rate for specific services, with a maximum limit on the number of hours that are authorized. In this way, you establish a fixed budget that can be exceeded only upon your further authorization. At the same time, make sure the person who will be assigned to your case is a full-time staff member so he will be available to testify if you need him.

Make sure, too, it is clearly understood that you are to be provided with written reports, and that you will receive itemized bills detailing the number of men used, the hours worked and the hourly rate for the service involved. Also, you should receive a detailed statement of additional expenses incurred.

One of my acquaintances who formerly operated his own investigative firm offers some added advice about charges.

> It is almost impossible for an investigator to take a case on a flat fee basis because he has no way of knowing, particularly if surveillance is involved, how many people he will need on the job or how long they will work. When you have a heavy, difficult auto surveillance, it is not uncommon to use three cars, and they must be equipped with mobile radios so you can alternate the close-in car. Two cars may be on parallel streets, or one might be the fifth car behind in a lane of traffic. You don't want to maintain surveillance too long with one auto, so you keep switching autos, which takes three good radio-equipped cars and three people. A client should receive an itemized bill, but don't be surprised if it's a big one.
>
> You should also insist that your bill list the names and license numbers of the investigators who were used. You are paying for trained investigators and you don't want the agency using wives or kids instead and then charging you the full rate for it.
>
> Sometimes, if the surveillance involves a husband and his paramour, you may have to use two investigators—one male and one female. If the husband's woman friend goes to the restroom, the investigators can split up so both subjects are still covered. But I've known cases where, instead of two investigators, the job is handled by one investigator and his girlfriend. You get one investigator for your money, plus another pair of eyes and legs, but you are charged for two trained people. If you're paying for two professionals, you ought to get two professionals. That's why you should insist on names and license numbers on your itemized bill.

Rule 5

Finally, make as certain as you can that your case will be treated in complete confidence. You should assure yourself that there is not the remotest chance the firm has any connection with associates or friends of your spouse or with his or her lawyer.

Following these guidelines could save you a great deal of grief, and a lot of money as well.

"Don't get trapped," Gene Allen says. "Follow the guidelines."

What to Expect from a Detective

What can you expect from your private investigator, once you've found him?

The answer depends greatly on the kind of problems you're faced with. Services will vary from case to case, for each is different. There may even be problems in your own case that are unique. The typical case, however, may use one or more of the following services.

Surveillance. A top-flight agency will be able to conduct a discreet surveillance of persons involved in your case. This will include reporting on the person's activities and contacts, minute by minute. "Shadowing" is an old-fashioned term, but that is what is done. A good surveillance report will include dates, times, places, addresses, names. These can be invaluable to you in the development of your case.

Character Survey. The agency can make a thorough investigation of the character and reputation of all persons involved in the case. Police records will be thoroughly checked in wherever the subject lived. Reports will be obtained on the reputation he or she has among business associates, neighbors and other acquaintances.

Associations. It is still often true that "birds of a feather flock together." Does the subject of your investigation hang around with members of the criminal element? With alcoholics? With drug addicts? A reputable private agency can answer these questions for you, in a factual way, without relying on gossip or hearsay.

Photographic Evidence. If this is called for in your case, the agency you choose should have expert photographers on its staff who are readily available to its clients. Amateurish, blurred photographs have ruined many cases that were otherwise airtight.

Responsibility for Children. As we will see later, the law can be grossly unfair on the subject of child custody. A good private detective agency can often dig out facts to support the right of the more responsible parent to gain custody of the children. Here again, the facts can cover a broad range: narcotics use, communal living without consideration for the children's health or well-being, alcoholism, even physical abuse of the children.

Impartiality. Some marriages are dissolved amicably but, more frequently, by the time a divorce is sought, the accumulated grievances of each party have stimulated feelings of hostility, rancor, and anger that make it impossible for either to view his or her situation calmly and dispassionately. Rational judgments become almost impossible. A good investigative agency, because it deals in facts, is better able to develop objective and convincing evidence to support your case. Later, if a member of the agency's staff testifies, he does so unemotionally, as a professional. He is trained to submit evidence in the courtroom in an objective, impartial manner.

Tracing. In a surprising percentage of cases, a husband or wife may move away without any warning, sometimes taking the children; the spouse's efforts to locate his missing mate and family prove fruitless. Skip tracing, thanks largely to techniques developed by bill collection agencies, has developed into a sophisticated science. An experienced investigator, without formality of a cap and gown, will have earned his degree in that science. In a vast majority of cases, he will be able to locate the missing person speedily and at a reasonable cost.

Occasionally, as Gene Allen points out, the decision to engage a private investigator may produce a surprise ending. If your real hope is for a reconciliation, a competent investigator may bring it about by dispelling false rumors or, perhaps, by uncovering positive factors that wash away the discord that brought the partners to the brink of divorce.

One wife became suspicious when her husband, who for years had arrived faithfully at the dinner table at 6 P.M. each day, suddenly began calling every Tuesday to report he had to work late and would not be home for dinner. After several such calls, the wife began telephoning the office on each of these occasions, but never received an answer.

Convinced that her husband was involved with another woman, she hired a private investigator to discover where her husband was spending his evenings out. Imagine her chagrin when he reported her husband went every Tuesday to a Little League ballgame with a fatherless boy for whom he had assumed the role of Big Brother. It was something the generous and sympathetic husband wanted to do, but he didn't dare tell his wife for fear she would resent his spending the time away from his own family.

The wife learned something about her husband, and also about herself.

Alibis

If a divorce complaint is filed against you, it may allege grounds that simply aren't true. You may, for example, be accused of adultery. It is difficult to prepare a defense against such accusations because a clever lawyer probably will not present details of the accusation until he has you at his mercy on the witness stand.

How will you deal with the situation if, as you sit nervously in the witness chair, one of the "dirty dozen" types suddenly asks, "Isn't it true that on the night of October 3rd you were in a room at the Starlight Motel with (if you're a man) Jane Doe?"

You will deny it vehemently, of course, because it isn't true. But such a lawyer will then ask, "Where *were* you on the evening of October 3rd?"

Your mind is blank. You sit there, aware of countless eyes upon you, trying desperately to recall where you were on the evening of October 3rd. You can't remember and become more frightened and distraught, not realizing that, if enough time has elapsed, few people could respond spontaneously to a question about where they were on a given, uneventful night. As one Chicago criminal lawyer told me, for some of his clients the best alibi is that they have no alibi. They didn't know they were going to need one.

Confronted with this situation, your best course is simply to answer, "I can't remember." Then volunteer that, if given the time and opportunity, you will check your records to determine where you were. And again deny having been in the motel.

The important thing is to remain calm and unemotional. Don't fidget or squirm in your chair or let your voice tremble. Maintain the demeanor of an innocent, falsely accused party. Don't be dismayed by counsel's vicious rhetoric as he badgers and bullies you. Offer to take a lie detector test. They are not admissible in court, but your willingness to take one may influence the judge.

Now consider how much more comfortable you would have been in this situation if you had prepared yourself for it. You knew from the original complaint that an attempt would be made to prove a charge of adultery. You knew the charge would be made more specifically once you got on the stand, but you had no way of knowing when they would allege the adultery ad occurred, or with whom. To offer an effective alibi in court, you would have had to reconstruct your life for a period beginning a year or two before the complaint was filed, and then try to remember every detail.

This reconstruction is a laborious exercise but one worth every minute you spend on it. If you keep a diary, go through it and reconstruct the last year or two of your life, day by day. If you don't keep one, check notations you may have made on your calendar about important appointments, visits to the theater or ball park, birthday parties, or other events. Then, recalling those occasions, try to recall what you did in the days immediately before and after each event. You will find it easier to recall where you were if you narrow the time frame and relate it to events that do stand out in your memory. If you have blank spots in your reconstruction, go over cancelled checks and credit card statements. These may yield information to jog your memory. Chances are, if you approach the task diligently and systematically, you may be able to develop a complete reconstruction of your life over an extended period of time. With this in hand, you probably will also find you can recall witnesses able to testify where you were.

Despite the effort you went to in developing the reconstruction, when you get on the witness stand you still may not be able to recall where you were when opposing counsel accuses you of committing adultery on a specific date. Don't panic. Remain calm and take your time. You won't have your notes—an old rule of law gives the opposing counsel the right to see anything you have in your hand. If he sees your notes, it may open up a new line of questioning. Leave your notes with your attorney and, if memory still fails you, ask for a brief recess to consult with him. You can then return to the stand and rebut the charges with detailed and specific information, and offer to present witnesses to prove it.

If you are in the early stages of marital discord but fear your problems may ultimately lead to divorce court, you can almost certainly profit from such reconstruction. Begin right now to keep a daily diary of events. Record in a notebook or on a desk calendar your phone calls, luncheon appointments and other social engagements. Maintain a complete and accurate record of where you spend your time. Record, also, the names of those you encounter, wherever you are. Phone calls may be important because, if it becomes necessary, you can check with the telephone company to prove you were engaged in a telephone conversation from a distant location when the lawyer says you were at the Starlight Motel.

If you want to be super cautious and you have a secretary, have her listen in on important conversations so she can verify that they occurred. You may even have her take notes. You can achieve the same result more simply by buying a miniature tape recorder with a suction or clip-on device that attaches easily to the telephone receiver. These devices offer the advantage of being portable. You can keep one with you and use it in your hotel room when you travel, or even on pay telephones.

Depositions

If your divorce case develops into a bitter, drawn-out battle, you may be required to give a deposition, the legal term for testimony recorded in a lawyer's office by a witness in a case. If you are unprepared, nervous or confused, you can severely damage your case while giving a deposition. Thus, some coaching is in order.

Your spouse's lawyer may ask the most hostile, demeaning, or insulting questions during the taking of a deposition. Be prepared for this. Keep calm, and keep your temper.

One man was asked by his wife's attorney: "Since your wife left you, have you kissed any girls? How many?"

The quick-witted husband was calm, alert and on his toes. He answered: "Dozens."

The startled but delighted lawyer pressed on. "Would you mind telling us just how many times and provide us with their names and addresses so we can check them all out?"

"Not at all," replied the witness. He then proceeded to recite a seemingly endless list of girls, explaining in each case that he had kissed her in the presence of dozens of people at an office party, or at a New Year's Eve party he attended stag with old family friends, or that the girl was the bride at a wedding, or the 10-year-old daughter of his business partner. As the recital droned on, the attorney's frustration became increasingly apparent and his temper began to rise. Finally, in desperation, he gave up, saying, "All right, all right. We've had enough of that."

What should you keep in mind if you must give a deposition?

1. *Stick to the point.* Offer no more information than what is required to answer the question. Volunteered information may set your opponent's lawyer off on a fishing expedition.

2. *Be absolutely certain you know the specific question* before you reply. If you're unsure, repeat the question out loud. Rephrase it, if necessary, and ask the lawyer whether or not this is what he is trying to ask. Or ask the lawyer to repeat the question so you may understand it clearly.

3. *Take your time in answering.* Collect your thoughts. Here again, if you need time to think, repeat the question or ask the lawyer to repeat it. And watch how the question is phrased. Don't let the opposition put words in your mouth.

4. *Don't be too helpful.* The opposing lawyer may make an assertion that is partly true and partly false and ask you whether or not it is true. Simply say "No." Don't correct his error by volunteering that it is partly true, because it may give him new information he can use against you. His errors are his problem, not yours.

5. *Tell the truth.*

6. *Don't express surprise* at any of the questions asked. Be prepared to have your personal life exposed like an open book. If you are asked a question you can't answer at the time, simply say, "I can't remember." Don't let your emotions give you away. Watch out for a quavering voice or body language that reveals your emotions. They may reveal to the questioner that he is nearing pay dirt.

7. *Be calm.* The opposing attorney may attempt to bully or badger you or try to get you to impeach yourself. Don't let these tactics frighten or intimidate you. Take your time and think carefully about each response. If a question is repeated, don't answer it a second time. Simply state that you have already answered it.

8. *Be cool.* If you react nervously to stress, you may wish to consult your physician about using a tranquilizer that will calm your nerves while leaving you mentally alert. It is important to remain calm.

9. *If necessary, ask your attorney if you can refer to your notes* or other sources of reference before you answer your spouse's lawyer. Chances are you won't be able to confer with your attorney before you answer, so it is wise to review your

personal notes before entering the deposition room and have facts and figures fresh in your mind. Remember the old rule of law; any notes in hand can be taken from you by the opposing attorney and used against you. He may learn from them more than you want him to know.

10. *Be correctly dressed.* Look, feel, and act the part of the righteous party. It won't show in the transcript, but it may intimidate the questioner—and it will help you psychologically.

11. *Know when you're finished.* The Supreme Court has ruled that a deposition may be taken only once, except in exceptional circumstances, such as the death of the court reporter before the notes have been transcribed. When a lawyer says, "I have no further questions of this witness," you are through. You needn't answer any additional questions.

12. *If you find you have incorrectly answered a question, correct it later.*

Witnesses

You may need more than your lawyer on your side. In some cases, it also helps to have witnesses. Some states actually require two character witnesses in every divorce proceeding. Your spouse, of course, may also present witnesses.

If your case is going to trial, your attorney may write your spouse's counsel and ask for full names and present addresses of any witnesses who will testify to the charges made in the original complaint.

When your lawyer receives this list, study it carefully. Do you recognize the names of any witnesses who could have seen, or actually did see or hear, what they presumably will testify to?

Assuming you are guiltless, be prepared to refute their testimony by referring to notes you gathered in your own investigation. Discredit their testimony whenever you can. Even if you don't know the witnesses, check them out.

In some cities, a witness can be hired for fifty dollars to support charges made by either side in a case. Your investigation may enable you to discredit a witness who is offering perjured testimony.

Evidence

In preparing your self-defense, it may be helpful for you to know what evidence is admissable in court.

Photographs. Photos should not have any writing or markings on either side. And remember our earlier warning: make sure you have duplicates hidden away in case the originals are lost.

Privileged Conversations. Ordinarily, private conversations between a husband and wife are privileged—unless someone else overhears them without the aid of a bugging device. The conversations then become admissable evidence.

A person could make an admission that, if overheard by a gardener, maid or repairman, could be used as evidence in court.

A lawyer discussing information with his client is engaging in a privileged conversation, as long as no one else is present. If someone else is there, the privilege is destroyed. The third party can testify as to what he or she heard.

Hearsay. The law of evidence makes hearsay inadmissable testimony.

6

No Man Is An Island

DIVORCE proceedings have a traumatic psychological impact on nearly everyone involved. Even if the decision to divorce is amicable, unmarred by the bitterness, hostility and rancor that characterize so many separations, you probably will discover that the absence of your marriage partner has left a huge void in your life.

Although you and your spouse may have decided to part simply because you were bored with each other, annoyed by each other's tastes or habits, or resentful of the restrictions and demands that marriage placed on your lives, each of you may soon discover that the adjustment to a solitary existence is not as easy as you had expected.

Not infrequently, separated husbands or wives soon begin to feel a sense of emptiness, not just over the loss of the cherished aspects of their marriage—and there always are some—but even over the absence of the things about their mate that annoyed them most. It is not surprising they miss familiar routines, long for accustomed surroundings, and become lonely because many of their closest friends, reluctant to identify themselves with either side of the marital dispute, suddenly neglect them both. But, oddly, they sometimes discover that marital disputes have become an important part of life, and some strong-willed spouses become desolate over the loss of their favorite scapegoats.

Women, abruptly alone with their children, have a particularly difficult time adjusting to that empty place at the dinner table, witnessing the sadness in the eyes of the children who at last realize "Daddy isn't coming home" and facing household ordeals their husbands once dealt with or at least shared.

The simple truth is that few individuals are so self-sufficient they can exist happily without the companionship of others. Yet many of those involved in a divorce—lonely, overcome with questions of guilt over the failure of their marriage, embarrassed and fearful of the evidence that may be dragged out in court—withdraw even further into themselves.

Don't let this happen to you. Divorce is a bitter experience for many, but it is not the end of the world. There is still a life ahead of you and it need not be an unhappy or empty one—unless you allow it to be. This is a time to reach out, to bid farewell to your melancholic island, to seek the aid and comfort of others.

Man is a social being whose own sense of worth is determined in the context of his relationships with others. We are enriched by our exposure to others, as they are enriched by their association with us. One person you once loved has gone out of your life, but this is not a time to wallow in self-pity. Bring some new friends in to share your rebirth with you. Instead of feeling sorry for yourself or surrendering to the apprehension that your future will be purposeless and empty, expand your horizons. Look for new people, new interests, new things to do.

How many times during the busy days of your marriage did you wish you had time for pursuits that interested you? Try to recall what they were: now may be your opportunity to pursue repressed goals and ambitions. If you are a woman, learn as much as you can about finances, home maintenance, personal grooming, cooking, planning or anything else that will make you more self-sufficient. Prove to yourself you can do most of the things you thought required a husband.

Most important, if you find it difficult to rid yourself of depression or if you still have reservations about the wisdom of divorce, don't be afraid to look for advice and help. The following pages will offer some suggestions on where to get it.

Conciliation

The judge's first question, when you and your spouse make your initial appearance in divorce court, probably will be: "Is this marriage over?" He will wait patiently while you and your spouse answer his question individually. Should either of you hesitate, he may recommend a different course of action than divorce. Possibly he will suggest that you obtain the counsel of a social worker or refer you to the court's conciliation service.

It is unfortunate that the judge is often the first person to urge a couple to try conciliation counseling. It should be every lawyer's first suggestion, but too often it isn't: lawyers view their clients as meal tickets, not as distraught human beings in trouble who need help. Most couples, too, view the filing of divorce proceedings as the end of the marriage rather than the beginning of a process that will determine whether or not it should be ended. They abandon any hope of reconciliation once the legal machinery has been set in motion, not realizing that the step they have taken is not irrevocable until the final decree has been signed.

A recommendation for conciliation counseling usually comes from the separation judge, the first jurist a couple sees in court. When he asks if you want to see a counselor, and one spouse is willing and says so, the judge may try to stare the other spouse into agreement. If the reluctant partner doesn't agree, the official court record will show that he or she was unwilling.

When and if the two partners decide to accept counseling, the judge will delay any motions on their case until they have met with the conciliation service. In some areas, this service is supported by the court; it is possible to use it only if you have started divorce or separation proceedings. Pursuant to the court order, your attorneys will arrange an appointment with the counselor, first together and perhaps separately later.

What occurs or is said in these meetings is privileged. Information is not supposed to flow back to the judge or to your lawyers, nor should the lawyers be present or attempt to influence either spouse. The counselor's function is to be neither judge nor jury. He acts as intermediary, posing questions for you to reflect upon. He will ask you how you resolve conflicts. He will try to get to know you and may be able to help you.

Such a counselor is apt to be bluntly honest and sometimes critical. You may be in for some rude awakenings or needed reassurances. The counselor may advise you that you are the more qualified parent and urge you to fight like hell to gain custody of your children, or he may tell you and your spouse that you should not have married in the first place, but that each of you might find happiness in another marriage to a more compatible person.

My session with a conciliation service helped me, not by saving my marriage but by raising my morale and encouraging me to develop more backbone. I became more determined in my purpose. I became more dedicated. Why? Because the conciliation service gave me hope. No matter your situation, a social worker or psychologist can often help you to view it more objectively and offer advice that could have a significant effect on your life. Approach the counselor with an open mind and you may gain a richer future.

The Honorable Charles J. Fleck, presiding judge of the Domestic Relations Division, Cook County, Illinois, Circuit Court is "convinced conciliation is beneficial. It can lead to couples discovering and understanding their problems. If a divorce is still inevitable, it can lead to a more lasting divorce and a better understanding. Their children will benefit. Fewer post-decree visits will ensue."

Couples with new insights into their new relationship sometimes choose to begin their marriage anew. They can cancel their litigation, reestablish their family, and, with a new outlook, try again. With a greater understanding of each other's needs and a spirit of mutual self-sacrifice the marriage often survives.

Psychological Counseling

Don't be surprised if your spouse's attorney asks that you be examined by a court-appointed psychiatrist. If he does, the court may decide that both parties should be examined. If you have any indication this is about to happen, be prepared.

First, check with knowledgeable sources and develop a list of reputable and unbiased psychiatrists so you can request an examination by a physician you can trust.

Second, when you see the psychiatrist, tell the truth. You have a right to your feelings, so don't be ashamed of them. Anger, disappointment or depression are probably normal symptoms of the trying situation you are in.

The psychiatrist may find that both you and your spouse are functioning normally or that one or both of you have some psychological problems. Should one partner need extensive therapy, the other spouse may be barred from obtaining a divorce pending completion of the treatment.

If you are required to seek additional counseling, don't be apprehensive. To take full advantage of a psychologist or psychiatrist's skills, you must be cooperative and candid.

What will it be like? If you see a therapist on a one-to-one basis, he or she probably will delve deeply into your past. He may ask why you married your husband or wife or try to help you conclude what you might seek in a future mate. His objective is to stimulate recall of thoughts, fears, experiences or feelings of guilt you have locked away in your subconscious mind. He's trying to help you know yourself.

If you choose group therapy, you will probably meet with couples and singles, divorced and married people. To break the ice, the doctor may ask someone to discuss his dreams, and he may explain something of what the dreams mean. Some couples will discuss conflicts, relating their difficulties in interacting with those who are close to them. You will soon learn your problems are not unique. Once you see how easily some of these problems can be resolved, or discover why you act as you do, you could be well on the way toward resolving your own conflicts.

If your conflicts are deeply rooted, you may decide to attend an extended number of sessions. But no one can force you to do so. Nor should you try to force an adamant partner to accompany you to group sessions; it probably will do no good.

Effective participation in group therapy requires an attitude of openness and candor that is lacking in those who attend against their will.

The important objective is to get your own head on straight. Then, thinking more clearly, you can decide what you should do about your marriage.

As I interviewed people for this book, I learned that a great many couples who undergo therapy do reconcile once they have learned to understand why their conflicts have occurred and how to avoid or handle them in the future. If you have a problem, seek help soon. You might reverse the cliche and turn a mountain into a molehill.

Other Sources of Moral Support

If you shrink from social workers and are fearful of visiting a psychiatrist, there's another person nearby who also is often well-qualified to help. He's your minister, rabbi, or priest. Some clergymen counsel couples themselves; some act as a trusted referral service to others who specialize in domestic counseling.

Couples sometimes avoid the clergy because they fear all they will get is a sermon about the sanctity of marriage and an admonition to go home and try again. In years gone by that often was the case, but today most clergymen, where marital differences are concerned, serve in the same role as the counselor or psychiatrist. Their purpose is to help you see your situation realistically, so you can deal effectively with the difficulties that confront you.

Whether you seek it from a counselor, psychiatrist or clergyman, or even from a wise and trusted friend, remember that help is there for the asking. If you have the wisdom and courage to open your mind and heart to any one of them, he or she may help you to change the course of your marriage or your life after divorce. But the time to seek help is early in the game, when the clouds of marital discord first begin to gather on the horizon. Everyone needs moral support at one time or another. To seek it may be one of the most courageous and rewarding actions you can take. But your attitude must be one in which you also want to help yourself.

7

What About Your Children?

CUSTODY fights, unfit parent, nonsupport, kidnapping, visitation violations, performance bonds, emotional scars—these are some of the ugly words and phrases that signal the potential impact on children of a decision to divorce. Too often, in the conflict between mother and father, the child becomes the battleground.

One of my most disquieting and often alarming observations about the hundreds of divorce cases I studied and the divorcing parents I interviewed was the frequency with which innocent children become helpless and bewildered pawns in the struggle between their parents. More often than I like to recall, hitherto decent and unselfish parents became oblivious to everything but their own bitter and often vindictive conflict with their mates, blindly visiting devastating emotional havoc on their children.

You and your spouse may have decided, despite the sacrifice it requires of your children, that they would be better off in a single-parent household than in one where they are exposed to the tension of constant conflict between the two people they love most. That may be a rationalization of the course you have chosen or it may, indeed, be true. In either event, however, both spouses have an inescapable obligation to make the divorce process as bearable as possible for the children.

If parents ignore or evade that responsibility, the children may bear the emotional scars throughout their lives. How well your children adjust to this unexpected and frightening development in their lives, one that shatters their tight little world and fills them with confusion and insecurity, will depend on the skill, love, selflessness and understanding with which both spouses handle the situation. Here are some things you should think about.

How Should You Tell Them?

Parents on the verge of divorce must put aside their own selfish concerns long enough to face together the awesome task of confronting their children and telling them the truth about what is soon to happen. "Your father and I both love you very much, but we are sure you have noticed we are unhappy living with each other. We are getting a divorce, but that doesn't mean you won't continue to see both of us. Remember, we still love you very much and always will . . ."

Difficult words.

But the school psychologists, ministers, psychiatrists, social workers, and loving parents I interviewed all agree that these difficult words, or others like them, must be spoken. Where and how you tell the children is also important.

Most children are more aware of the stresses and strains that have existed in their household than many parents know. The longer you delay explaining the facts of your situation, the more likely it is they will begin to harbor dark, unnecessary fears—"We'll never see Daddy again"—and imaginings—"Mommy doesn't like us"—that often will be more emotionally damaging to them than reality itself.

Who Should Tell Them?

Psychologists generally agree that both parents should discuss their plans with the children. If the parting is exceptionally bitter and the parents cannot, even for a few minutes, subordinate their own interests and concerns to the welfare of their children, one parent may have to take the responsibility. In that event, it may help if another person close to the child—a favorite teacher or close relative—joins in explaining the situation.

What Should You Tell Them?

Psychologists recommend that parents agree in advance on exactly what the children will be told. The children should not be confused by hearing two different explanations, nor should they be burdened with accusations and counteraccusations that force them to take sides or try to assess who was to blame.

Keep it simple. Communicate in words the children can understand. Acknowledge that you are incompatible, but don't demean your future role as parents by flinging accusations at each other and trying to force the children to judge who is right and who is wrong. Instead of talking about the love that was lost between you as their parents, stress the love both of you still feel for them. Reassure them this will always be so. Don't let them feel they will have to make a choice between loving one parent or the other, or be denied a continuing relationship with both of you.

Finally, it is vital that your children be made to understand they bear no responsibility for the conflict that has developed between you, their parents. Unless they are convinced of this, children often suffer horrible feelings of guilt because they believe they are in some way responsible for Dad's departure or, in other cases, Mom's. If you fail in your responsibility to prevent this guilt, your children may be emotionally damaged for life.

When Should You Tell Them?

Tell them as soon as possible after the decision has been made, preferably while the family is still intact. Your children will be far more upset if they learn of your plans from a neighbor, or through overheard gossip, or are taunted about it by a playmate. In that event, they probably will be afraid to ask you about it, and, in their fearful imaginings, they will create a vision of their future more disturbing than the one that will actually exist.

Timing may also be important. Don't begin this traumatic discussion just before bedtime or at a time when your child will soon face something like an important exam or departure for camp. Pick a time when each child can digest the information and then, later, have an opportunity to question both of you about any concerns he or she may have.

How Will They React?

The reaction of children to the news their family is falling apart is impossible to predict. Sometimes they ask many questions. Be ready with answers that will reassure them as much as possible about their future. Make it clear they will be seeing Daddy on weekends and during the holidays, or that Mommy really loves them but right now feels she must go away for a while.

Other children may react with apparent indifference, which is often an indication that they are rejecting reality in the hope that it is only a bad dream that will have gone away when they wake up. If so, it is your job to help them accept the situation for what it is and adjust to it with minimal apprehension.

Finally, don't leave it there. Take advantage of the services of school counselors to check on how your children seem to be adjusting. The noncustodial spouse, especially, may want to take advantage of this opportunity. Since he or she will not be in daily contact with the children, school personnel offer an effective means of monitoring the children's adjustment problems.

For many children, divorce means that their world, as they have known it, is flying apart. Now, most of all, they need a renewed sense of security, and reassurance that both of their parents still love them. Parents who deny them that—however obsessed they may be with their own shattered hopes—deserve nothing but contempt.

Who Will Get Custody?

Children should not be treated as part of the spoils of divorce, to be divided up like furniture or won like alimony. Yet, many of the most vicious battles fought in the divorce courts are over the custody of the children.

One of the professionals I interviewed does home studies and investigations, on court order, for a major metropolitan area. Here are her thoughts about the plight of the children of divorcing parents.

> Divorce need not be traumatic in the extreme if both parents are cognizant of some of the factors and their effect on the children. I think that parents can do a lot to help children accept divorce. One of the most important things is to help them understand that, while now there will be two households, both parents still love them, and that the children have a right to the love of those parents.
>
> I believe, too, that the emotional impact on children depends on the process they go through. Parents are often involved in a bitter conflict. Frequently this bitterness is encouraged by our divorce laws and judicial system, and also by attorneys who manipulate parents and often involve the children in this manipulation.
>
> The divorce laws, except in no-fault states, require that two people be adversaries. That is part of the problem. In addition, children are used as pawns in the final settlement negotiations, even in the no-fault states.
>
> In the last few weeks, I have been working on a case in which the father, at the time of the divorce a year ago, fought bitterly for custody of his teen-aged daughter. It was finally agreed that the couple would have joint custody, with physical possession of the daughter given to the father, while the mother would have physical possession of the son.
>
> Since then, the father has remarried, and a tug-of-war has developed between the daughter and her stepmother. The father now absolutely refuses to have the daughter continue to live in his household. However, he is about $1,900 in arrears on his payments to the girl's mother, and his attorney does not want him to surrender the girl to her mother until the mother agrees to waive the payments due her.
>
> Rather than taking the child out of the father's home immediately, as was recommended after a home visit, the father's attorney insisted she remain. The result was a needless tragedy: the daughter ran away, got involved in drugs and, apparently, in prostitution.

But the fault here was not only that of the father and his attorney. The mother's attorney did not act to have the child removed, because he felt this would prejudice her case: she wants to collect the child support due her and also to deny the father the privilege of visiting the son, who has been living with her. She is overwrought because the son gets so upset when he visits his father. I think she is simply being protective, and that it is the attorney who is doing the manipulating.

Manipulation of clients by their attorneys is not unusual. They will often manipulate the oldest sons in order to get a good settlement for the husband. I had one case in which the father told me his attorney had advised him to upset his son and get the son to act out, in the presence of his mother, his wish to refuse to go to counseling sessions and his dislike of the Catholic school he was enrolled in. The boy, wanting his father's approval, was a nervous wreck.

Perhaps this is repetitious, but I can't stress it strongly enough. I believe that couples who fight over custody are still involved in their own battle, which began when the marriage turned sour. Too often, when visitation and custody are matters of contention, it isn't because either of the parties has the welfare of the child at heart; both are simply using the children as weapons in their own dispute. The law should be changed to protect children who are the victims of this kind of situation.

There are four basic types of custody.

1. *The mother has custody.* This is the most common, probably because a vast majority of judges believe that the mother is better able to raise and care for the children.

2. *The father has custody.* In the past this was rare, but today increasing numbers of tenacious fathers are winning the right to care for their children.

3. *Both parents have custody.* This is known as joint or split custody; the divorce decree recognizes the competence of both parents to raise the children.

4. *Neither parent has custody.* Both parents are judged incompetent to care for the children, who become wards of the state or a guardian.

Mother's Custody

There was a time when courts almost automatically granted

custody of minor children to the mother. Some unscrupulous attorneys, their minds fixed on earning another handsome fee, still tell their female clients they can "guarantee that custody of the children will go to you." Many women, for whom this proved to be an empty promise, have told me they would not have considered divorce had they known they would risk losing their children.

But times are changing, and so is child custody. As more fathers assert their right to custody, it is only the unprincipled lawyer who will lure a client into divorce proceedings with the empty guarantee that he or she will get the children.

In most cases, courts still rule in favor of the mother, even when the father is the more qualified parent. But when a father can prove the mother is unfit to care for the children, he has at least a fighting chance to win the custody battle.

And, a new trend is developing. "More women seem to be giving up custody of their children to the fathers," says the Honorable Robert L. Hunter, retired presiding judge of the divorce division of the Cook County, Illinois, Circuit Court.

Some of these women choose to relinquish custody because they don't really like children or don't want to be burdened with them. They may already plan to remarry, and the future husband has no rapport with the kids.

But often the decision is made for unselfish reasons. The father may be better able to provide for the children. He can afford a house in the suburbs, vacations and the extras of life. On her much smaller income, the mother, even with alimony and support payments, realizes that she will have to struggle to make ends meet. If she assumes custody, she knows she will deprive the children of advantages they could have enjoyed. Then, too, many women who married when they were too young find that they cannot cope with running a household. They know the demanding challenge of rearing children alone is beyond them and conclude that they can be better "weekend mothers" if they have some time to recapture the lost years of their childhood by rediscovering themselves during the week.

Father's Custody

An Illinois father recently petitioned a post-decree court for the custody of his children. He won. It was the first case in the state's history in which a father obtained custody of his children without proving their mother unfit.

In most cases, the only way a man can win custody of his children is to prove that their mother is unfit to provide proper care and supervision. These are tense, unhappy court battles, but fathers can and do win some of them.

One man won his fight to care for his young children when his wife admitted to the judge that she allowed them to smoke marijuana cigarettes. She also admitted she often left them alone for several hours at a time with only a telephone number where they could reach her. That judge awarded custody to the father. But another, in the same circumstances, might have ruled otherwise.

Proving that a wife is an unsatisfactory mother is often more difficult than this. But fathers who despair over what may happen to their children in the custody of an unfit mate, and are determined to gain custody for themselves, can find allies for their cause. They can check with the children's pediatrician and keep their medical histories. Are they often ill? Do they have evidences of emotional or physical disabilities that are the consequence of their home environment? Has the doctor found any hint of mistreatment or neglect? Have their teachers and school counselors observed any changes in the children that indicate neglect on the part of the mother? Is their attendance regular? Have their grades suffered? Do they come to school looking unkempt and in need of adequate rest? Neighbors, too, can often provide similar information.

It's an uphill battle, but more and more fathers are winning it. If you're a father, you may, too. But, if you love your children, don't become embroiled in a traumatizing battle for their custody without first honestly considering whether you are fighting for their welfare or your own. Will they really get better care and upbringing in your custody, or are you simply exploiting an opportunity to get even with your wife?

Joint Custody

If you and your mate can put aside your individual desires for redress of the wrongs you feel each has done the other and can give primary consideration to the welfare of your children, consider the possibility of joint custody. This arrangement offers a number of advantages to parents and children as well.

Under joint custody, the children are apt to live with their mother, but their father retains a strong voice in their upbringing. He is legally entitled to be consulted about education, summer plans, and other aspects of their intellectual and physical growth. And, if anything should happen to their mother he has custody without further court action.

When Custody May Be Changed

Suppose a husband or wife discovers that the custodial parent is neglecting the children or that they are not adjusting well to life in their new situation. This could happen to you, and you should be aware of what you can do.

Consult with your attorney and decide if you want to return to court to seek a change of custody. Decide if you really want custody of the children, and if you are financially, emotionally, and physically able to care for them full-time. If not, a foster home or a guardianship might be better for the children than to leave them in the care of a negligent parent. This may also be a temporary solution to their problems, especially if your situation makes it impossible for you to assume custody now but you expect it to improve at a later time.

If you decide to seek a change in custody, a welfare investigation is in order. You need credible witnesses to prove neglect and that the behavior of the custodial parent is unfit.

What type of neglect justifies a change in custody? Consider the case of a father whose wife and children lived with her bachelor brother. The brother worked all night and the wife played while he worked. She habitually returned home at seven in the morning and so did he. Meanwhile, the children were alone in the house, dirty, unfed, and unattended. The brother/uncle, a decent man who liked the children, was disturbed and disgusted by his sister's neglect of them. He arranged for witnesses to observe the mother's lack of care, and the father, who had remarried, sued for and was granted custody of the children.

Neglect is the most common, but not the only, condition that causes judges to rule in favor of a change in custody. A change may be made when (1) a custodial parent interferes with the visitation rights of the ex-spouse, (2) either party remarries, or (3) a change of circumstances occurs, such as loss of employment, ill health, or a mental breakdown.

I know of one recent case in which a mother persistently refused to allow her ex-husband the visiting privileges that had been ordered by the court. The judge finally held her in contempt and ordered her to serve ten days in jail. She has now been released from jail but is continuing to refuse her husband the visiting privileges that are his right. The probability is that her stubbornness and defiance will ultimately result in her loss of custody and award of custody to the father.

Custody should never be taken for granted, for the judge's original decision is never final. There is no such thing as permanent custody. The children are under the protection of the state. A petition and a stroke of a pen can change custody. Being aware of some of the reasons why judges will make these changes may help you to retain custody—or to regain it.

The Honorable Charles J. Fleck, presiding judge of the Domestic Relations Division of Cook County, Illinois, Circuit Court strongly believes: "Judges are viewing leaving the jurisdiction with less leniency today. With the high mobility of society creating greater and greater problems, it essentially terminates the parental relationship between the noncustodial parent and the child. The courts are really going to have to look closer at these requests as one parent figure will be removed from the child's future development. And this will strongly affect the best interests of the child. A child needs identification with both masculine and feminine figures. If a child grows up with one parent, that child grows up with a lot of emotional problems. Parents must have an awareness of this to solve the problem. The problem is that in the past, judges have viewed present effect on the best interests of the child instead of viewing the future psychological and emotional effects and the best interests by reason of the absence of a father or mother figure in that child's life."

8

Financial Angles

A divorce court judge once told me, "Man is the only animal that can be skinned more than once." If you study it carefully, the information in this chapter may save your hide.

Divorce not only taxes your emotional resources but, while your defenses are down, it also often confiscates the bulk of your financial reserves. Much of the advice given here will be of primary benefit to divorcing husbands who are the sole breadwinner in the family. But if yours is a two-income family, or one in which the wife has significant assets of her own, she also will benefit from being accurately informed about the financial aspects of divorce.

In Chapter 2, I offered some advice on protecting your assets prior to the filing of a suit. If you took it to heart, you are already better prepared to face the settlement negotiations. If you didn't, and a divorce action is already in progress, this chapter is your second line of defense.

In divorce cases, three financial elements are of primary concern to the attorneys. These are the future financial needs of the client, the income of the client, and the assets of the couple. If you are a salaried person, you can be sure your spouse's attorney will examine your Form 1040 with the zeal of a bloodhound from the IRS. If he is diligent, he will investigate to determine if all exemptions claimed are legal and if any retirement or profit-sharing benefits are noted. He will look for evidence of savings plans, stock or bond holdings, and insurance coverage. He will try to determine whether or not you have reduced your taxable income through the use of tax shelters. If your income and assets are substantial, and your sources of income and claimed deductions numerous and complex, he may have your financial condition audited thoroughly by a C. P. A.

Nonsalaried spouses who are self-employed can expect investigations of their real estate holdings, depreciation write-offs, expense accounts, and gifts made to reduce large capital gains. The opposing attorney will look for evidences of affluence and extravagance. Do you employ domestic help, own a second home, maintain an apartment for business purposes, or own a recreational vehicle or pleasure boat? He may inspect your business payroll, to learn if it includes a mistress or member of your family who are not actually doing any work. He may also examine your business inventory, to learn if it has been understated in the declaration of your assets.

Your capital gains and losses will be subjected to painstaking scrutiny, as will notes that you claim are outstanding or loans you have made to others that you declare as uncollectible. The lawyer wants to ascertain whether or not the debts you claim are real and the monies owed you really are uncollectible. If you have assets in trust, he will examine those to determine how he can get his hands on them. If you live in a state with an income tax, those returns will be scrutinized as well, because they sometimes reveal information not included on the federal return.

Finally, both lawyers will want sworn statements ot your assets and income. Don't fence yourself in by providing a statement that is more specific than necessary. Keep all the latitude you can for future negotiations.

As you enter the settlement negotiations, bear in mind the

critical importance of spelling out in clear and precise detail every aspect of your agreement. Don't risk the possibility of future misinterpretation of the agreements you have made. Don't sign an agreement that leaves any questions up in the air, or you can bet they will come back to haunt you.

All too often, men are so eager to get the legal proceedings over with that they take the quick, easy way out. They accept the terms that are offered them and fail to make sure they have not accepted undefined and unmentioned future liabilities. Those who are this impatient and careless often discover, in later years, they have enrolled themselves in a school of hard knocks where the tuition is unconscionably high.

However completely you may trust your attorney, don't allow yourself to forget that even the good ones survive on the fees that emerge from marital disagreements. The bad ones foment many of the disagreements themselves, at the couple's expense. If you fail to exercise caution in the negotiation of the final settlement, you may get a liberal education billed by the lawyers at Ivy League tuition rates.

Don't let the lawyers draft settlement agreements that are loosely written and leave important questions hanging. If you do, you may be plagued forever by multiple interpretations or misinterpretations. Chances are you and your ex-spouse will find yourselves back in post-decree court. Remember, the lawyers don't mind. For them, your plight means additional fees. Your bread is their butter, and it's a high-priced spread.

Alimony

The word *alimony* derives from the Latin noun for food or support and the verb "to nourish." These roots make clear its original purpose. Unfortunately, over time, it has assumed a new meaning and, in comtemporary divorce proceedings, it more often stands for fiscal retribution or reparations for marital warfare than for basic care.

Couples with the wisdom and judgment to perceive divorce as the basis on which they can build happy, solvent, independent futures for themselves will avoid employing alimony as a punitive device. They will regard alimony as it should be regarded—a temporary means of supporting the wife while she takes care of minor children or gains the needed skills to support herself adequately.

There are several ways to make alimony the financial resource that nourishes a new, independent relationship. By spelling out the terms of alimony in the final decree, spouses can anticipate future contingencies and avoid depleting their assets because of attorney's fees assessed for post-decree court appearances. Now is the time to consider alimony's variations.

Term Alimony

Although regarded by many vindictive spouses as a means of retribution, the real purpose of alimony is to enable the wife to become financially independent. Unless exceptional circumstances preclude the possibility that the wife will achieve financial independence, alimony payments should be of limited duration. However, if alimony is required as a permanent arrangement for such reasons as physical or mental inability to become self-supporting, a minimum standard guarantee should be considered.

In recent years, one of the most popular arrangements has been the five-year guarantee of alimony with an extension of up to a ten-year maximum if the ex-wife has not remarried. If she remarries during the extension period, the alimony terminates. This plan has several significant advantages. It encourages the man to accept his ex-wife's remarriage without resentment and gives him an incentive to fulfill his alimony commitment without the oppressive knowledge that he may face a lifetime of payments to an ungrateful former spouse. Meanwhile, it is an incentive for the woman to develop the skills she needs to become independent, because she realizes her alimony will not go on forever.

Without limited term alimony, an ex-husband and wife are eternally bound together by financial commitments. They have abandoned their nuptial bed but in the process created a new financial bed that both will have to lie in. Continued dependence on her ex-husband is demeaning to the wife and often a financial nightmare for the husband.

Too often husbands, in their desperate eagerness to resolve their marital problems, accept unlimited alimony commitments that will haunt them for the rest of their lives. That can be a very long time, and it becomes longer with each passing year. G.D. Searle & Company, a leading pharmaceutical manufacturer, predicts that by the year 2000 the normal life expectancy may increase from the present 72 years to 90 years. A couple who married at age twenty-one in 1976 and divorced in 1980 could remain "married"—by alimony payments—until the year 2045. Imagine being saddled with alimony payments for sixty-five years!

No Alimony

Most men resent the award of alimony to their ex-wife, feeling—justifiably in many cases—that both partners were responsible for the failure of the marriage. However, if the judge finds that the wife has grounds for divorce, or if a no-fault decree is granted, alimony probably will be awarded unless there has been a previous agreement between the parties that does not provide for it or provides for a cash settlement in lieu of alimony.

An exception may be the case in which the husband proves his wife was at fault. In such a case, the judge may award child support to the wife but withhold alimony. Support payments are awarded regardless of fault, because the court's primary concern is the future well-being of the children. This is not the case with alimony payments.

As the thrust for women's liberation has gained momentum, an increasing number of independent women have rejected the concept of alimony. They feel that their own self-esteem is enhanced if they demonstrate their independence from their former husband and prove they can stand on their own two feet. For them, acceptance of alimony is a chain that binds them to their dependent past.

The proud woman who shares these convictions should be wary of her own attorney, for he probably will press her to demand alimony despite her own convictions about it. Divorce lawyers don't like their clients to renounce alimony because it damages their track records as they search for future clients. More important, they are aware that if they get larger financial settlements for their clients they can demand fatter fees.

In many states alimony is now considered spousal support, meaning either gender can have support or maintenance.

Reserve Alimony

A woman may simultaneously salvage her pride and protect her future by asking for reserve alimony instead of demanding it immediately. If a woman signs a decree not containing a provision for alimony or reserve alimony, she is forever prevented from obtaining alimony. A reserve alimony clause reserves her right to obtain alimony through the court if her circumstances change and she then needs financial support.

Automatic Escalator Clause

If the wife's situation is such that alimony is justified on a continuing basis, it is wise to provide in the decree for the possibility that the payments may require upward adjustment in the future. If no such provision is made and the husband's financial circumstances improve, or the wife's needs increase, or continuing inflation has reduced the value of the alimony payments she receives, another trip to court will be required to make the necessary adjustments.

If the couple spells out in the decree an automatic escalator clause that allows for equitable adjustments in the amount of alimony on a clearly defined basis, it may save substantial sums in the long run. Many men prefer this arrangement because it enables them to plan more effectively, eliminates the need for costly court appearances and legal fees, and spares them the necessity of taking time off from work to visit court and losing income that may result from their absence. Women like it because it gives them greater peace of mind.

Remarriage Clauses

Divorce laws in some states include automatic stipulations regarding the payment of alimony when the ex-spouse remarries. If the laws of your state don't include such provisions, be sure to delineate clearly in your settlement agreement the circumstances in which you will continue to pay or receive alimony. Should a man continue to provide financial support for his ex-wife while she lives in the home, arms, and life of another man? Does an ex-wife have a right to continuing compensation for years of service rendered?

If you look to the origins of alimony, the answer is clearly no. Alimony and child support are intended to provide financial assistance to the extent it is required for the support of his children and necessary support for his ex-wife until she can become financially independent. It should not be used as a punitive device to burden the husband, prevent his remarriage, or provide an unrestricted subsidy for his ex-wife. If the husband's financial position changes, for better or for worse, so should his financial obligations to his ex-wife. This also applies to changes in the financial circumstances of the ex-wife.

For example, assume that a divorcee with several children and minimal income from child support marries again. If her new husband is a man of average income, she may be required to work full-time to help her new husband support children who are not even his. If financial adversity strikes, this unfair burden on the new marriage will create a dreadful strain. It appears doomed from the start. The woman cannot take care of her own children properly, begin a new family with her second husband, and also be a scintillating bride. Meanwhile, the financial condition of her ex-husband has improved dramatically. Doesn't he have an equal and continuing obligation for the support of his children? Should he not be required to free their mother from the burden of full-time employment?

And what of the divorced man who remarries while he is still obligated for substantial alimony or child support payments, or both? This combination could mean a bleak future for his new marriage. Alimony, when there is a failure to define clearly the legal and social responsibilities involved, may create an insurmountable barrier to the husband's prospects for eve achieving a successful second marriage.

Other possibilities also need definition. Suppose a woman

remarries a man she believes to be wealthy. He dies unexpectedly and she discovers that he has a very small estate. If her first husband did not stipulate that alimony would terminate on remarriage, or if the state law did not make such a provision, she may still be entitled to it. In the years of the second marriage, her ex-husband, although still obligated to pay alimony, may have stopped making payments. She did not object while her second husband was alive; but now, with a renewed need for support, she goes to court to force payment of back alimony and continuing payments in the future.

Unless a couple meticulously defines the countless contingencies that might arise, they invite future trouble for one or quite possibly both of them. What's fair in love and divorce? Can you expect all concerned to be fair?

Alimony and Child Support Guidelines

As a rule of thumb, a man can be expected to pay 20 to 30 percent of his net income to his ex-wife in alimony and 20 percent for child support. However, the latter will vary according to the number of children and their ages and needs. In setting the amount, the court will also be influenced by the amount of income available to the husband.

Under federal income tax regulations, alimony is treated as a deductible expense for the husband and as taxable income for the wife. Child support is neither deductible for the husband nor taxable for the wife, but if the husband can prove he is providing more than half of the support for a child, he can claim an extra deduction on his tax return. If the judge orders a single monthly lump sum payment that combines both alimony and child support—"alimony in gross"—the entire amount is deductible by the husband and taxable to the wife.

Finally, a word of warning: the Internal Revenue Service requires that alimony payments be written into separation agreements in order to be deductible. A reference to alimony in court records and other documents is not sufficient.

Reducing Alimony

Alimony doesn't have to be a permanent ball and chain.

When the circumstances of either husband or wife improve or decline, it is possible to raise or lower alimony payments by returning to court. Better still, provisions for automatic adjustment of payment under specific circumstances can and should be written into the decree.

Take the case of the man who failed to plan his divorce and include such a stipulation. After a time, his greedy ex-wife began eyeing his salary. His attorney told him that if she went to court she could probably get an additional 25 percent of that salary, above the amount he was already paying. To avoid this, he voluntarily increased his alimony payments by forty dollars a month.

Six years after the divorce, he has discovered that his ex-wife has two jobs, a new Volkswagen, a new color television, and new furniture, and has moved into a more expensive apartment. He is extremely bitter because he hasn't enough money to build a life of his own. He can't afford to remarry. The lawyers will prosper if he heads back to court to try to have his alimony reduced.

In another case, the decree granted custody of the children to the wife and provided that the husband would pay her $100 a month in alimony and an additional $100 for child support. Subsequently, custody of the children was transferred to the husband, and his ex-wife went to work. He then went to court with the request that the alimony be terminated and that the wife pay *him* $100 for child support. However, he gave the judge the option of holding the question of child support in abeyance, pending his ability to send the children to college in future years.

The judge granted his request for termination of alimony but denied the request for immediate child support. He did, however, hold the child support question in abeyance to enable the husband to return to court if financial assistance from the children's mother is required when they are ready for college. This case demonstrates that, increasingly, courts are recognizing the responsibility of both parents for the support of their children. Wives as well as husbands may be required to contribute child support.

It is also well to remember that judges are human, too. Some of these concepts are new and unfamiliar, and if you include enough demands in your request that there is room to negotiate, you may get most of what you desire. A judge likes situations in which he or she can grant something to each of the parties so they will feel their attorneys won something for them, and that the judge was wiser than Solomon.

Alimony Row

Alimony, because it involves a continuing relationship between two people who have already demonstrated their incompatibility, generates some of the bitterest battles of divorce. Be prepared for unfair play or you may end up on "alimony row." Although it is late in the 20th century and debtor's prisons are presumably a thing of the past, ex-husbands still may become alimony jailbirds. Pay up, on time, by check so you have a record of it, or you may find yourself behind bars.

The *Chicago Tribune,* on August 29, 1972, reported the story of a man celebrating his wedding dinner with his second wife, their friends and relatives, when he was interrupted by the sheriff. He was handed a writ of attachment alleging he was in arrears in child support payments for his son. He was unceremoniously hauled off to the local courthouse and spent his wedding night in the county jail.

The law and the courts generally have little sympathy for men accused of failing to support their children. This antipathy can be, and often is, exploited by vindictive ex-wives who, even after the decree, remain bent on revenge. More than one husband has spent a night in jail, accused of being in arrears on support payments that actually had been made.

The psychological and financial havoc that can be inflicted by a malicious former spouse is sometimes beyond belief. Consider the case of a dentist in a prosperous Midwestern suburb who was brought to financial ruin, and his reputation and practice destroyed, by a divorced wife who was not content with taking most of his money.

The terms of his alimony were clear. He was to pay $1,100 a month for unallocated alimony and child support, from which his wife was to make the monthly mortgage payments on the family residence, which she would occupy. She was awarded custody of the children, with specified visiting privileges for the father.

Although the dentist's financial commitment was substantial, he was relieved to have the matter settled. Or so he thought, until his ex-wife's harassment began. Shortly after the court order was entered, he began receiving bills from the mortgage company for the monthly payments. His wife, although required to do so, was refusing to pay them and had instructed the mortgagor to bill him at his new address. Rather than risk losing the house, he paid the bills.

His next problem arose when he attempted to exercise his visiting privileges. His former spouse refused to allow the visits unless he paid her sums of cash in addition to the alimony she had been awarded. During those visits it became clear that she had been systematically poisoning the minds of his children against him.

During the ensuing weeks and months, there followed an incredible campaign of personal harassment. The wife called his office employees and tormented them with accusations that they were having affairs with her ex-husband. She called his patients and urged them not to pay their bills. She began cruising through his neighborhood in the evening, spying on him and his neighbors and even sending one of his children to peer through his windows. On one occasion she followed him in her car, repeatedly crashing into his rear bumper at stop signs or when he was slowed by traffic. He complained to the police, but when they discovered that a domestic problem was involved, they refused to act. She then began sending anonymous complaints to the various state regulatory authorities, accusing the dentist of charging exorbitant fees and of having illicit relations with his female patients. Soon the dentist found he could not retain his employees, was losing his patients, and was having difficulty in collecting from those he had treated. The loss of income, coupled with the excessive payments being made to his wife, brought him to the brink of financial disaster.

At this point, his ex-wife had her attorney file a complaint in court that the dentist was in arrears on his alimony payments. In fact, his records and cancelled checks proved he was paying her substantially more than the required amount, but no matter.

"I was in my office treating a patient," the dentist recalls, "when a police car drove up outside with its lights flashing. The police ran around to the back door to guard it, I suppose to keep me from escaping. Two sheriff's deputies came in the front door and presented an order for my arrest. I peacefully went along with them.

"Although I made no effort to resist, they shackled me and led me out of the office, on a bright summer afternoon in full view of all my neighbors, and took me away to the police station. Later they took me to court where the judge said, 'Let's see what happens if he spends a night in jail.' "

At 4 P.M. the paddy wagon arrived. It was a hot day. The dentist was hauled off to jail with thirty other prisoners, was photographed, fingerprinted, stripped and searched and, finally, incarcerated with hardened criminals, drug addicts, and an accused murderer. Ultimately he was forced to pay more than 50 percent of his income to his ex-wife, plus the mortgage payments.

Why?

One reason may be that the ex-wife's attorney was better known in court, which gave credibility to his charge that the dentist was in arrears—the judge refused even to look at his cancelled checks that would have proved otherwise. Why didn't the man's attorney fight for his client? That question is still on the dentist's mind today. His experience has convinced him that there is an alimony row, but not that there is justice.

He has since been jailed a second time, with equally demeaning consequences. Today he is virtually without income and is deeply in debt.

The most paradoxical aspect of this case is the misery the ex-wife herself has endured because of her obsessive desire to gain revenge on her husband. When her ex-husband stopped making the mortgage payments for her, she actually let the house go to foreclosure. She and the children were evicted, their possessions piled up on the street. She then called a television news department and was photographed with her children, standing in the midst of their possessions and blaming her ex-husband for their plight.

The case is still in the courts.

The moral to be drawn from the dentist's experience is clear. If a husband who believes he has reached a fairly clear-cut settlement with his ex-wife can undergo an experience like this, imagine the potential fate of anyone who accepts a settlement that leaves basic questions unresolved. It also demonstrates the unmerciful reaction of many judges to husbands they believe to be in default on their court-ordered responsibilities to their children.

Although such cases are uncommon, it should be noted that a husband's responsibilities to his children can also be extended to his second wife. In one case, a wife agreed to step aside so her husband could marry again. The final decree stipulated that the first wife was to receive alimony and child support for a minimum number of years.

When the husband's second marriage ended two years later, he was $9,000 in arrears on his alimony and support payments to wife number one. Since he worked only intermittently, chances were slim that he could ever pay up.

The first wife and her attorney decided to look to wife number two as a source of funds, and sued her for the back alimony and child support. The judge ruled in favor of the first wife.

Child Support

When the mother becomes the custodial parent, child support is awarded almost routinely to ensure that the children will have at least a minimum of support until they reach legal age or are otherwise emancipated. As the need for advanced education has increased, so has a growing tendency on the part of judges to award support for minor children even past the 18th year. This seems appropriate if the child desires further schooling and has the capability to benefit from it. In some cases, the child may also have need for exceptional schooling.

In awarding child support, the judge endeavors to meet the minimum needs of the child with provision for further amenities if the father is financially able to provide them. The court recognizes that a mother alone with the children may be unable to work. Child support bridges the gap until the children are of age, or at least until they are old enough that the mother can obtain employment.

Alimony is a negotiable element in any final divorce settlement; child support is not. It is a matter of public policy that a father must provide for the support of his children.

Nonetheless, child support also has become one of the explosive issues that bring couples back into post-decree court.

A recent study by the Chicago Chapter of the National Organization for Women revealed that one in four divorced fathers in the Chicago area does not comply with court orders to pay child support. However, life may become more difficult for fathers who desert their families and fail to support their children in the future. A new federal law authorizes the use of federal courts, IRS collection procedures, federal data files and garnishment of federal salaries and retirement benefits to enforce child support requirements.

Here again, an ounce of pre-divorce preventive planning will be worth years of post-divorce wrangling in court.

Monetary Arrangements

Child support can be for a minimum figure if the wife has given her spouse ample grounds for divorce. A judge will often reduce the wife's requests if the wife is vengeful and destructive. If the mother restricts or hampers a father's visitation rights, the judge may modify the child support payments.

The wife may usually spend child support funds as she sees fit, which may not always be for the benefit of the children. Many men want to end future obligations to a wife by agreeing to a lump sum. There are advantages to payment of a lump sum in lieu of alimony, but this option may not be wise in the case of child support, particularly if the wife has demonstrated that she is a poor money manager and is likely to make unwise investments. If your wife dissipates the lump sum settlement you gave her before your children reach their majority, you still could be held responsible for their support.

There is the added hazard that lump sum settlements are apt to attract the interest of any lawyer involved in the case. If the cash is in an escrow account or the lawyer's own account, he may be exceedingly reluctant to part with any of it until he has contrived a bill tailored to the amount to be received by the wife. This temptation is minimized if the settlement provides for installment payments.

The woman who is young, attractive, has few children and the hope of remarrying may wish to remain independent of alimony. But she should not reject child support. If and when she enters into a second marriage, its chances of survival will be enhanced if her new husband is not required to provide full support for another man's children.

Even if the wife does not request immediate child support, she should exercise the option to reserve or table the question of child support for future determination. If it is left open in the settlement decree, it can be reopened at a future date. This choice can be made for many reasons. A custodial parent does not know how much it will cost to raise the children in the future; or she or he may be in a hurry to shed mate number one so she or he may marry number two, who is waiting in the wings; or the couple may not have enough money to pay the legal counsel to settle all the items necessary. They may not have good legal representatives who can help them avoid the pitfalls that lie ahead. However, they should realize that reserved items are subject to future negotiations and post-decree appearances, and that these will result in future legal costs. The matters that can be reopened should be spelled out as completely as possible to keep future costs to a minimum.

Arrearages on Child Support

Every parent should be aware of an important appellate ruling regarding unpaid child support. The court held that arrearages on alimony, and some other disputed items, may be waived at settlement and decree times. But child support must be paid. In one case, a mother was granted retroactive child support payments dating back fifteen years. The court ordered the father to pay, even though the ex-wife had made no effort to collect the payments due over all those years.

French Leave

Bargain to avoid having to come to this crossroads. Men subjected to exorbitant financial settlements sometimes skip town and disappear after placing their assets in a trust or a foreign bank. The children suffer. An unreasonable and oppressive settlement that takes an unconscionable percentage of a man's income isn't worth anything if it causes him to split. The wife and children are deprived of support and the children of the love of their father.

One Minnesota man decided to take French leave after negotiations with his wife and her attorney reached an impasse. Their terms were so outrageous that he asked his attorney what to do. His lawyer replied, "If you are still here on Tuesday, we'll have lunch together." Notice that the lawyer did not specifically advise his client to skip; but the implication was there. The man did not show up on Tuesday. He gave most of his personal belongings to his nephews, packed what he could carry, and left. They haven't heard from him since, and the wife who drove him to it has yet to get a dime from him.

Most men do not find such drastic measures necessary. But French leave is a last resort for many.

Automatic Reductions in Child Support

Avoid post-decree costs by writing a fair and equitable settlement formula now, before the final decree. Automatic clauses will provide protection for the warring spouses. These clauses can spell out conditions that may arise in the future and will modify stipulations now being made. If you are reluctant to pay more now to write an ironclad agreement, remember that it may save more substantial costs in the future.

A husband should insist on a stipulation that, if the custody of one or more of the children is awarded to him at some future time, the payments for their support will automatically cease, pro rata.

He might also seek a stipulation that, in the event his ex-wife is working and he gets custody of the children and isn't well off financially, she also may provide a certain amount of child support.

He may stipulate an automatic reduction as each child reaches eighteen, does not go to college and becomes self-supporting. Careful attention to details may raise your legal fees now but usually are the cheapest in the end. Don't leave anything for future misconstruction or interpretation.

Visitation Reductions

Don't overlook the opportunity to reduce child support payments by eliminating them during the vacation periods your children spend with you.

An Accounting of Support Money

If your wife is vindictive and greedy and petitions for an increase in child support, consider filing a petition of your own, for the same court date, asking for an accounting of her expenditures. It will save duplication of fees, and a psychological advantage may be gained. She may be profligate in her spending habits or lavishing money on her own desires at the expense of the kids. If you petition for an accounting of support money, you may be able to prove that she is not as destitute as she claims, or even that she is neglecting the children.

Division of Property

If you escape bitter battles over child custody or alimony, it may be the dispute over who will get the convertible or Aunt Jan's antique chair that will do you in. The spoils of divorce are often material, and husbands and wives who do not seek vengeance on each other often find that their lawyers have divided up the material products of their union.

It doesn't have to be that way. Try to be fair, and, if fairness isn't met in kind, at least be aware of your legal rights and options.

Community Property

Community property states usually divide equally any property acquired subsequent to a marriage. These states include Arizona, California, Louisiana, Nevada, New Mexico, Idaho, Texas and Washington. If you don't live in a community property state, you must negotiate a property settlement through your attorneys, usually before your case comes to trial.

Several factors affect the division of your worldly goods. If one party paid for an item, chances are he or she will retain it. If title to property is held in the name of the spouse who did not pay for it—for legal, tax, or business reasons—that spouse may not get automatic title to it in a divorce. An obvious example is a home deeded to the wife so that, in case of her husband's death, she would have a secure title to their home without obligation for inheritance taxes.

A nonworking wife may have a difficult time proving that property is hers. A working wife is more likely to have receipts and canceled checks to show that possessions were purchased with her income. If a wife bought the house with her own money or money inherited from relatives, she must be prepared to prove the source of her funds. If checking or savings accounts hold money she has saved from her household budget, she'll very likely have to prove that, too. Any income and assets she has at the time of the divorce must be accounted for at that time.

Pots and Pans

Customarily, upon divorce, the woman has been given most of the personal property. She usually has been allowed to claim the wedding gifts, shower gifts and the pre-wedding gifts as her own, and often the home and its furnishings, as well.

Frequently, the man is brainwashed into thinking this is the way it has to be. He is probably told by his lawyer that he shouldn't deprive his children. He may name twenty or twenty-five items he wants if she'll let him have them. But the wife will decide if he can have them or not. It's a degrading and humiliating exercise. To add insult to injury, the husband is usually required to pay the legal system that separates him from his hard-earned assets.

Since very few single people make an inventory of the possessions they bring into their marital partnership and too few married people keep one during their married years, the division of personal property is difficult, frustrating, and often grossly unfair.

Reasonable people will preserve their assets by agreeing to an equitable division of their worldly goods and avoiding a costly and frustrating encounter in "pots and pans" court. Confrontations of spouses over relatively insignificant possessions have destroyed more settlements, wasted more lawyer hours, and run up more needless bills than almost any other aspect of divorce. I have been in courts where divorces have been held up interminably while the judge determines who is to get the marital bed. One item! The legal costs were more than the bed was worth. Judges also deputize lawyers to go to the house, observe and report back to the judge. This increases your legal fees, too.

Besides, no judge has the time or patience to sit on the bench dividing up thirty-six single-spaced pages of items. Nor is this process a reliable way to protect your rights to a favorite possession; his decisions are almost certain to be arbitrary and capricious.

If you and your spouse can't agree, you may have an arbitrator—a lawyer or another qualified person—help you. This method is costly and you are bound by his decision. You may have an option of refusing the first arbitrator, but you won't have much more latitude.

Finally, there is post-decree "pots and pans" court. Most lawyers hate this system, which delays the settlement and postpones the day they can collect their final fee and get on to the next case. Others like it because it can run up courtroom fees. One lawyer told me he can make clients become so sentimentally attached to an old, torn dishrag that they will litigate over it. Some lawyers are masters at drawing these things out and running up bills.

Consider some of these guidelines for winning your fair share of your possessions. First of all, if you think you are doomed to litigate each piece of silver, don't stipulate in your final decree that property will be divided equally or evenly. If you do, it's likely that a post-decree court judge will zip through your list of possessions and assign ownership to you or your spouse with little regard for equity, sentimental considerations, or value. Instead, merely state that property is to be divided before a post-decree judge within a certain time period. Then you have a fighting chance.

Before you appear in court, plan your strategy. If you have a wedding gift list, this can help prove which side of the family each gift came from and help establish the right to the item.

Another deciding factor you may want to establish is need. If you can show that your mate has a coffeepot, toaster, vacuum and a supply of toys for the children, the court very likely will recognize your need for these items too, if there are duplicates.

Plan your phrasing carefully, too. Be firm in your demands, but don't appear unwilling to accept reasonable compromises. Avoid such words and phrases as "always" and "never." Appear reasonable, and you will win the sympathy of most judges. Finally, beware of the judge who will try to intimidate you into accepting an unfair distribution of property. One of my friends was almost sold down the river by a judge in a hurry to get to the golf course. His ex-wife had a long list (single spaced, in elite type) of what she wanted. Fixing the husband with a hostile stare, the judge began by announcing that he would award to the wife the crystal and silver. The husband objected and his attorney, who had never faced this judge before, broke in with a question. "Your honor," he asked, "are you a magician?" The judge was so startled he didn't reply at once, and the attorney smoothly went on to explain that the litigants were in dispute about many of the items on the wife's seven-and-a-half page list. "It will take a magician," he said, "to divide these things up in a reasonable period of time."

The judge, still eager to get to the golf course, asked the attorneys to step into his chambers. The husband's attorney then suggested that instead of the wife's list, it would be quicker and more equitable to use the Bride's Book, apportioning the items to the spouse whose family or friends had been the donors. He noted that items in the Bride's Book would take care of ninety percent of the contested list. The judge was relieved. He promptly suggested the lawyers decide on a formula out of court before they met again. Any items not decided by then could be decided by him "his way." Court was adjourned, the judge had his golf game—and ultimately a reasonable settlement was reached.

While pots and pans distribution can proceed more smoothly within the framework of some general formula, do not allow your lawyer to commit you to a formula or agreement without your specific consent. He doesn't know which of your possessions you value most and, in his eagerness to get the case over with, he may cause you to lose items you might have won.

Real Estate

A house, apartment or vacation home may be a man's castle, but almost invariably it is the wife who gets to call them home after a divorce. Since it is the propensity of courts to rule in favor of the wife in the case of real estate, a divorcing husband must be prepared for a particularly bitter fight if that four-bedroom colonial or A-frame is the possession he wants most. Recently, men are winning the right to live in the home they bought with their mortgage payments. But to have a fighting chance will take shrewd planning and good legal advice from the very start.

Should You Move Out?

It's usually a psychological victory to stay in your own home and may be a legal mistake to move out. All too often, a man is forced to move out of the family homestead when divorce looms. He is brainwashed into believing that he will lose it anyway, so he might as well give up and leave. He may be receptive to the suggestion because of the anguish of living under the same roof with a warring wife. Then, too, the judge at the initial court appearance often talks turkey to the lawyers and suggests that he is going to order the husband to move out of the house.

Here is where a man's lawyer can prove he is worth his salt. A fighting attorney will tell the judge his client is not moving out. He stands a chance to stay if the wife has not given any grounds for her divorce. He must not have physically abused his wife or even threatened to strike her. He must be made to appear the wronged party to win this round. Sometimes, if the husband can prove the wife and children have nothing to fear from him, the judge will let both parties remain under the same roof.

Unfortunately, the wife's attorney may then salve his own ego by telling the wife to move out. He will promise to get her back into the house alone shortly and, meanwhile, force her husband to pay separate maintenance, which she cannot get while living in the house with him.

Generally, this is poor advice. Unless her life is threatened, the wife should endeavor to stay in the home. The one who leaves voluntarily will almost always have a hard time getting back in.

Does Title Establish Your Squatter's Rights?

Title, theoretically, determines the legal rights to property. But in divorce cases, title often is not a clear-cut determining factor.

The title to your real estate may be held one of several ways. Joint tenancy is most common for marital homesteads. But it can be tenancy in common. It may be in your individual name or in a trust or corporation.

Those owning real estate prior to marriage may still hold it in their own name alone. In some states, subsequent to marriage they can sell it without a partner's signature. In others they cannot, and the result often is grossly unfair. The other spouse, without any equity in the house, can prevent its sale and sometimes win possession of it when the marriage splits.

However, the courts have recognized in many cases that property owned prior to marriage—i.e., a home—can indeed revert back to the original owner. A single person contemplating marriage, who plans to use his or her equity as down payment on a house, should consider purchasing it prior to marriage. All is bliss now, but who knows? There may be a subsequent divorce.

What if Someone Slaps a Lien on Your Property?

An ornery mate or anxious lawyer, fearing he won't be paid, may place a lien on your property. The lien clouds your marketable title. Don't stand for it. Try to have your mate or that lawyer pay for the removal of the lien. It will cost you hundreds of dollars otherwise.

A lawyer may have good reason to fear he won't be paid. But with all the legal terminology available to him, a carefully worded document assuring he will be paid for bona fide work can or should substitute for a lien. Suggest it as an alternative.

Selling Property

A decision to sell your home is one of the many by-products of divorce. Before you put up the "For Sale" sign, you should be acquainted with some of your alternatives. And if you still decide to sell, at least observe some principles that will make it easier for you.

The first thing you should decide is: do I have to sell? Maybe you want to make a lump sum settlement, instead of paying off over a period of years. Too many men get panicky. They have one major asset, their house. Lawyers encourage home sales to assure the proceeds will pay their fees and, often, little is left over for the little woman. It can be stupid to be railroaded into such action.

Often it is possible to save your real estate. How? You may consider raising the mortgage on it. You can refinance it and get a second mortgage if your credit is still good. Relatives may co-sign notes to shore up your credit rating. Why not rent it? Wisely chosen tenants who pay sufficient security deposits needn't ruin a property. With inflation, the value of the property will almost certainly increase. It will be easier to pay off the mortgage with inflated dollars.

Look for an alternative that will give you time to reach a carefully considered decision. Don't sell when you are under strain. Another possibility is to rent the house to your spouse for a set number of years. It may encourage her to stay nearby and ensure your opportunity to see your children. If your wife pays rent, you can use the maintenance and real estate tax deductions and depreciation to give yourself an income tax break.

If the alternatives of renting or refinancing do not work out, you may be forced to sell your home and/or other real estate. But, again, consider the protective devices you should bring into play. A smart couple will determine which of their respective lawyers will perform the legal services required to dispose of this property, and demand that this service be performed without an additional fee. In addition, record all expenses incurred so that when your decree says "net proceeds" you can deduct these costs from any amount owed your spouse.

Be certain that the final settlement decree specifies, if real estate is to be sold, who chooses the broker/lawyer and who will determine and pay for expenditures for repairs to ready the property for the market. It should provide for reimbursement of these costs off the top of the proceeds from the sale.

Do not let your spouse's counsel embarrass you at the closing of the sale of your home. To avoid the humiliation of a cigar-chomping bagman, ready to scoop up the proceeds as part of the divorce settlement, do this: allow only the real estate person, the real estate lawyers, and the buyers and sellers in the closing room. The divorce counselor who represented your former spouse in the divorce has no business being present. He has no right to know all the financial details and should be content to wait outside to be paid.

Another wise precaution is to limit your spouse's access to your property before its sale. Vengeance can wreck more than your peace of mind, as one suburban husband found out. Before his wife vacated their home, as required by their agreement, she held a rifle and shotgun party. The day after revealed broken windows, chandeliers, shattered doors, and bullet-ridden walls. The husband sustained enormous costs for repairs before he could sell the house.

After the divorce and the sale of the house, the couple was again in a post-decree court because the man felt that his ex-wife should pay the damage. She claimed she was away at the time and had no knowledge of the party. The fact that the woman had the care, custody, and control of the house during that time should have made her responsible. A properly worded agreement in separation would have covered and protected this contingency, but instead additional lawyers, court costs, etc., had to be paid. The lawyers did not do their job.

A comparable New Jersey case made the papers in 1976, but this time it was the wife who was upset. Eugene Schneider, of Carteret, New Jersey, was being sued for divorce by his wife, Phoebe, on grounds that he "would constantly and continuously bring women into the marital home."

Mr. Schneider was upset, as many others have been, with provisions of New Jersey's divorce laws requiring fair and equitable division of property. He undertook to administer the statutes literally by using a chain saw to try to cut his $80,000 house in two.

Other husbands would probably give Schneider an award as the divorce court "fighter of the year," but his wife didn't see it that way. She promptly filed additional charges against him for malicious damage to the home.

Insurance

New husbands, new fathers, brides and expectant mothers usually think a great deal about insurance. Divorced couples do not. But divorce is another watershed, a time to protect the future. Stipulations regarding insurance, therefore, are an important part of many settlements.

Car Insurance

When one partner leaves home, he or she might take the better of two cars or take the only car. In either case, the spouse left behind may well need a new car or a better one. My advice is, let your spouse buy his or her *own*. If you buy the car and place it in your own name, you'll be obligated for car payments and insurance. In case of accident your spouse could cripple or kill another or others and you could be sued, perhaps bankrupted. No thanks. It is simple prudence to avoid these costs and risks.

Life Insurance

Give careful consideration to life insurance stipulations when it comes time to draw up your settlement terms. Generally, one side or the other will insist that the existing policies be maintained "irrevocably," with the wife and/or children named as irrevocable beneficiaries, either permanently or until they reach their majority. Consider demanding a stipulation that a trusted relative be designated as the administrator of your insurance estate. This would add some assurance that these funds would be properly spent for the education and care of your children. State in your will whom you would recommend to be the guardian.

Consider using your paid up additions to reduce the cost of your premium. These are the times when you probably need all the additional cash you can muster; if you can reduce your expenditures, it will ease the financial pressures. You can also raise cash by withdrawing the paid up additions to the policy, thus reducing it to the original face value.

Husbands should also be wary of the tax consequences of insurance settlements. Let us assume the husband agrees, as part of the settlement negotiations, to carry insurance on his life naming his ex-wife as beneficiary. If the husband follows the IRS rules, the premiums he pays can be considered as alimony—tax deductible for him and taxable income for his wife.

This applies, however, only if the wife is the sole owner of the insurance policy and the husband's obligation to maintain it has been spelled out either in the written settlement agreement or in the divorce decree. If the husband assigns the policy voluntarily, without being required to do so in the written agreement or decree, he will not be able to claim the deduction.

Social Security

Social Security means financial security for some, but if you are divorced, you may lose your right to it. Check carefully on what it takes to qualify in your individual situation and make sure your settlement fulfills the requirements, if possible. Many wives who have been faithful for decades have lost this protection simply because they and their attorneys failed to check the rules.

Medical Insurance

The mounting costs of medical, dental, and hospital care have prompted many wives to fight for stipulations that the husband will be liable for all extraordinary medical expenses. All too often, the man is hooked because he has overlooked his best defense. This is the simple but eloquent fact that the wife is one of the parents, too. She should be equally responsible for the medical and dental health of the children. Frequently, parents do not have the individual resources to pay extraordinary medical bills, especially those of a catastrophic nature. It should be a joint responsibility.

One way of assuring in the settlement that both parents will shoulder medical expenses is to require that the custodial parent pay the deductible sum usually required by the medical insurer. This stipulation will help to ensure that every ache and hurt doesn't result in a trip to the pediatrician for a fifteen-dollar Band-Aid or aspirin tablet.

Also consider ruling out payments for certain optional categories of dental and medical care, such as orthodontia or psychiatric care. Psychiatrists can charge from thirty to seventy-five dollars an hour, and these bills can continue for months or years. You, as the ex-partner, may be stuck with them. If a partner has required psychotherapy while you are married, it is possible that you will still be liable for the bills after the divorce, too. Divorce can cause all kinds of problems in children, too. Take care!

I am focusing on these things to help you write the best possible divorce settlement. Know your family and yourself. Consider your willingness to participate in their future care and the extent to which you can and should contribute. You have a life to live in the future. Should you remarry, and your ex-wife or husband keeps you broke, it may destroy your own future happiness.

Divorce attorneys are quick to put something in writing about medical bills, and judges get used to stipulating that the husband must pay them. All too often, this becomes a permanent responsibility. Medical bills incurred before the separation might ordinarily be paid by the husband. But medical bills incurred subsequent to a spouse's leaving should be open to negotiation. You don't want to deny your children adequate medical care, but you should avoid giving your spouse free rein in the area because she has escaped all responsibility for the costs of that care.

Insurance and Tax Deductions

Remember, if you get stuck with payments for abortions, birth control pills, and vasectomies prescribed by a doctor, IRS now considers them deductible. Also, in the case of life insurance policies where a wife is an irrevocable beneficiary, tax courts have recently ruled premium payments by an ex-husband are considered alimony he can claim as a deduction and the wife must report as income. Be sure, however, that this requirement is spelled out in the settlement or final decree. I repeat, the voluntary assignment by the husband will not satisfy IRS rules.

Taxes

For most men, at least, divorce is a financial disaster. Just as Uncle Sam provides disaster relief for flood victims, he allows some tax relief for divorce victims. Now is a good time to be alerted to some of the tax implications of any legal actions you take in securing your divorce and writing up the settlement terms.

Joint Returns

Is there one more joint return in your future? If you are still in the process of divorcing, consider the advantages of having your spouse's signature on a joint income tax return. Not only may it reduce your tax, but these are sworn statements. If your spouse later attempts to question in court some of your declarations about your assets, you have his or her signature to certify the accuracy of your accounting.

On the other hand, you should be aware of the disadvantages of filing a joint return. If you are paying temporary alimony, it cannot be deducted on a joint return. If you file a joint return and are entitled to a refund, the government check will be in both names and cannot legally be cashed without both signatures.

If income tax time is near and your spouse is balking at signing a joint return, file an application for an extension on the individual tax return. You will probably receive a sixty-day extension. If your spouse has taxable income and has not filed, she or he will be in default and will weaken her or his own bargaining position.

The tax consequences of divorce can be extremely complex and vary widely from one situation to another. To gain the best advantage, check your own case with a good accountant or with the Internal Revenue Service.

Tax Errors

Sometimes, in the emotional stress and strain you are going through, you may make a mistake on your tax forms. Check with the Internal Revenue Service; it probably will tell you simply to file an amended return. Don't be too concerned with honest mistakes. Most taxpayers make them.

Tax-Deductible Legal Fees

The money you pay either your own or your spouse's attorney is nondeductible when you have been billed for services rendered in connection with a divorce. But there is a legal way to deduct a portion of the legal fees. If you can arrange it, have the legal charges divided into two separate bills covering the total amount owed. One statement will cover the charges for the divorce itself. The other will cover fees for investment counseling in relation to real estate and/or securities investments and business affairs.

Deductibility hinges on whether the legal expenses were for

carrying on a trade or business, or for managing, conserving or maintaining property held for income production. Any smart lawyer with the help of a C. P. A. can figure out how to word correctly the time and money spent on his services for other purposes than a divorce. The important distinction is that the legal advice would have to be oriented toward income-producing activity in order to be a deductible business expense.

A nonworking woman may find an attorney's fees incident to a divorce as necessary expenses for producing or collecting income under Code Sec. 212(1).

The courts also have held that legal fees allocated to legal advice on tax consequences deriving from property settlements and alimony in divorce actions are deductible as expenses associated with determining an income tax liability. (Code Sec. 212(3)) If, after a divorce is final, a person sues to obtain a settlement, such as an ex-wife suing for property, that portion of the legal fees may be deductible. It all depends on the suit. If the main proceedings originate as a divorce, it is not deductible. The taxpayer must be seeking profit activities. The IRS frequently quotes the Commerce Clearing House for interpretations. You can check Code Section 212 on legal expenses.

There is so much a really reputable attorney can do to help minimize the financial burdens of a divorcing pair, if only he would. But he may not bother to apportion the exact time spent on the legal and the financial-counsel parts of his bill. In that case, you can help yourself by keeping those earlier-mentioned accurate, notated and diaried records on the talks or discussions you have with your attorney. Note the specific time, date, place and what you discuss. Carefully separate these notes into taxable and nontaxable classifications. If your lawyer will not cooperate with you, check with your accountant as to what reasonable portion of your lawyer's charges the IRS will allow you.

The IRS will want paid receipts for any deductible expenses. Therefore, pay by check and note on the check the type of legal services it covers.

Property Settlements

Do not agree to a property settlement or a lump sum settlement in lieu of alimony without first carefully exploring the tax consequences. While alimony payments are deductible for the husband, lump sum payments may not be—a fact that might influence the husband's decision. Check with your tax attorney, C. P. A. or the IRS.

Medical Dependents

If something happens to one of your children in the future, you could have medical bills running into the thousands of dollars. If the injured or sick child has an income of more than $600 from earnings or trusts, IRS precludes anyone from claiming him as a dependent. However, the child can become known as a "medical dependent." Form 1040 instructions will show allowable deductions. These should include commonly accepted medical deductions, such as prescriptions, aspirin, Band-Aids, dentists, doctors, psychiatrists, hospital charges, even travel ordered by a physician for reasons of health.

Disinheritance

Divorce actions can be a little like shooting craps. Usually, even if you have studied the game, you need Lady Luck on your side. Sometimes you need more than luck. You need extra financial leverage. The threat of disinheritance can sometimes be a powerful lever. It may have sufficient force to enable you to swing a better bargain.

I know of one man who didn't just threaten, but promised his wife he wouldn't lift a finger to talk his relatives out of disinheriting him. He wanted fair treatment for himself and his children before he would approach his relatives to ask them to reconsider. This loss of inheritance for the husband, and especially for the children, can have a tremendous impact on a greedy wife. She is intimidated by the knowledge that her children may find out some time in the future that her vindictiveness caused their financial loss.

So, should you have a money-hungry, vindictive spouse who has threatened you with endless reprisals, explain your problem to the possible benefactors. Do not ask them to disinherit you. But they might see the prudence of such action as a means of preserving the assets of the family.

It may be misconstrued that you put the relatives up to it. It must be very clear that you did not.

If there is a possibility that your children may receive an inheritance, while still minors in the custody of your ex-wife, you might ask your relatives to set up a trust for the children. You don't want her to spend their inheritance.

Making Payments

In the hurry to get the financial pain over with, few people pay sufficient attention to how they handle both temporary and permanent payments for alimony and child support.

One pitfall husbands should avoid is paying their wives' bills through the wife's attorney. What often happens is that the wife's lawyer calls the husband's counsel and says he's sending over her bills for collection. The husband's attorney will then include a charge for handling these bills as part of his fee. Ask your attorney about these arrangements and be sure he knows you do not want this method of payment.

You should carefully monitor expenditures of your wife for which you are held responsible. Some wives obtain greater subsidies from an unsuspecting husband by obtaining an agreement for reimbursement for the purchase of clothing or other merchandise. After she has been reimbursed, she returns the goods to the store and pockets the cash.

Ex-wives deserve the same kind of protection from negligent husbands who fail to make support payments. They can gain it, not by having the payments made through the lawyer, but through the court.

The method of having monthly checks sent to a court clerk involves an extra middleman and delay, but it also alerts the court to possible nonpayments and discourages husbands from falling in arrears. You might consider this stipulation in your settlement decree if you suspect that your spouse might fail to pay or flee the jurisdiction. The influence of court involvement may also induce him to pay on time.

Out-of-Country Payments

Another consideration in regard to payments is the use of foreign currency in cases where one or both spouses live abroad. Settlement terms may provide for payment in local currency instead of in dollars. Remember, fees are levied for the exchange of one currency for another. Moreover, devaluations and fluctuations in exchange rates may increase your costs. If I were the man whose wife is overseas, I would endeavor to specify that alimony and support payments will be based on American dollars.

Rebuilding Your Credit

By the time the divorce is granted, one or both spouses have often shattered their credit rating. It will take time to rebuild your credit, but it is possible. Often, department store credit managers will restore limited credit privileges if your delinquent bills have been paid and you carefully explain the circumstances that caused you to become delinquent. Then, as your rebuild a record of prompt payment, you can have your credit limit increased.

Know that you have the right to examine any credit company's file on you. If you have been refused credit because of information in the file, there is no fee. Otherwise you pay a nominal charge.

Recent federal credit legislation limits the time during which derogatory credit information can be maintained in your file. Once this information is outlawed, and you have established a record of payment with two or three accounts, you should be able to have full credit privileges restored.

9

Your Day in Court

SINCE the moment divorce became an impending reality, rather than an ugly word in your vocabulary, you've been headed for your day in court. As the time of your first court appearance approaches, fantasies may begin to appear in your dreams—visions of hostile jurors, menacing judges and conspiring attorneys. This section may not give you the courtroom composure or the strategic skills of a Perry Mason, but it may help you face with some degree of equanimity your day or days in court.

If television has formed your image of the learned man on the bench, he probably has silvery hair, a fatherly face, an even disposition and a fierce devotion to justice. Prepare to be disillusioned: the ideal is not always reality. Before you go to court, study the attitudes of real-life divorce judges in and outside the courtroom. Then try to put your case in the hands of a judge in whom you have confidence.

Change of Venue

To do this may require a change of venue, the legal term that describes changing the location or judge of your trial. It is a maneuver you can use to try to make certain your case is tried before a fair-minded judge.

Cases in most large jurisdictions are usually assigned by the chief judge of the particular court. If you have done preliminary scouting before your case is assigned, you will have some idea of the attitudes and fairness of the judge. If he's not completely acceptable, you can exercise your right to a change of venue, which will remove the case to another jurisdiction, or you can ask for a bill of substitution in order to get a different judge. But remember, you get only one change of venue. So don't request it frivolously, because there is always the danger that the second judge will be worse than the first. You can ask for the change but you can't select the substitute.

How to Judge a Judge

How do you weigh a judge's sense of justice? What should you look for? What are the signals that should warn you a particular jurist may be less than judicious?

Observe the judge's behavior in court. Does he appear interested and concerned, or does he act like a disinterested spectator? Is he satisfied with perfunctory and unconvincing testimony, or does he press the witnesses to support their allegations? Does he appear to favor some attorneys and deal unfairly with others?

Pay close attention to everything the judge says during the course of a trial. You may discover that he appears to be unduly friendly with one of the lawyers. If it is the lawyer who will be representing your spouse, beware. And don't be content with courtroom observations. Spend some time in the courthouse hallways. Observe the attorneys with the judges when they are off the bench. How friendly are they with each other?

Talk to the clients and get their opinions of the lawyers who represent them. Be discreet and diplomatic, but learn as much as possible from those whose fate is already being determined by the court

If your jurisdiction has elected judges, try to determine whether or not some lawyers or law firms have provided substantial campaign support for any of the judges. There is nothing illegal about it, but it is reasonable to assume that such support may wield an influence.

All of this will help you to weigh your attorney's opinion when he says a judge is good or bad. If you have seen that judge in action and your attorney feels you can't get a fair trial in his courtroom, you may agree to ask for a change of venue. Whether you do or not, at least part of the decision will be yours—if you have done some careful investigating. You'll be one step ahead of clients who leave all of the decisions to the gods and the lawyers.

Should you decide to accept the judge assigned to your case, he still may not be the one you face. The other side has a change of venue open to it, too. In most cases, however, unless you or your spouse objects violently to him, your case will be heard by the judge originally assigned to it. Lawyers usually accept the judge who is dealt to them because they don't want to prejudice him against them in future lawsuits by objecting to him in your particular case.

In Chambers

When you make your first court appearance, the judge will probably invite the lawyers for both sides into his private office, or chambers. His purpose is to discover what the parties are demanding and what they may reasonably expect to receive. But he also may attempt to force one side to agree to unpalatable provisions in order to reach a settlement out of court.

Later, the judge will meet privately with you and your attorney to discuss your desires. In this meeting he may indicate whether or not he considers your expectations unreasonable and advise you on how the law applies. Usually, if you appear to have fair, reasonable, and proper objectives and stick to your guns, the judge will be sympathetic. Of course, he may not be. If you find yourself in conflict with the judge, don't count very heavily on your attorney for moral support. Lawyers fear arousing the wrath of a judge; rarely will they contradict one in a direct confrontation.

It is wise to remember that judges are human and that those who have spent much of a lifetime on the bench inevitably get jaded and bored after years of listening to other people's troubles. You may think the indignities you have suffered are unique, but you can be sure they're not. The judge could recount cases that might make you believe your marriage is a pretty good arrangement, after all.

Often those who have been on the bench the shortest length of time have the most compassion and concern, simply because their work is new to them. They haven't heard everything. One divorced man recalls with amusement how he explained his situation to a divorce judge who was new on the circuit. The judge, meeting with him in chambers, said, "There are two things I can do for you today. One is to grant a divorce. The other is to save your financial skin. What do you feel you can comfortably give your wife?"

The surprised fellow named a figure he thought was reasonable. The judge looked with distaste at the voluminous case records he didn't want to wade through and asked if the man couldn't do better.

"After all, you did have the use of her services for seven years," the judge said.

"Yes, your honor," the man replied quickly, "but she had the use of my services, too. And I was even more generous. I shared her with dozens of her boyfriends."

The judge laughed and agreed to the original figure.

The Judge's Orders

Whenever you appear before the judge, even to determine something as elementary as visitation rights, be sure you pay close attention to everything he says. He may tell you, for example, that you can have the children on weekends between certain hours. These may be firm or flexible hours and days. But you may also have requested flexible and variable additional hours for such special events as birthdays and vacations. If he has ignored this request, raise the issue while you are still in court, because the position he takes will become part of the court record when it is written up on his order. You will get your rights spelled out in the order—no more, no less—and these will be the ground rules you will have to live by.

After your case is adjourned, wait around to pick up a copy of the judge's order. Watch out for sub rosa maneuvering by your opponent's attorney. Sometimes the judge's words change their meaning between the bench and the typewriter. Wait for a legible, handwritten or typewritten copy of the order and read it carefully to be sure it interprets the judge's orders as you understood them. It is far better to raise questions then and there in court before the lawyers and the judge. Otherwise, it will cost you additional time and money to return to court to resolve misunderstandings.

It is also wise to get the name, address, and telephone number of the court reporter taking notes on the proceedings. If a dispute arises, you can pay a fee to acquire a verbatim transcript of the testimony and the judge's rulings. You may have listened carefully to the judge and know that what he said was in your favor, but the lawyers may have failed to reflect this in the written order. Keep them honest and force them to include every concession that was made in your behalf.

I have witnessed many instances in which lawyers have deliberately omitted specific rulings from the final order. One of the parties who won important concessions from the judge lost them to his opponent's lawyer. The judge has to sign the order, but don't count totally on him to read it with great care before he signs it, or even to recall without prompting the rulings he made in court: your case was probably but one of many that day. Don't submit to the lawyer's deception. Speak up and hold out for everything the judge has said you have coming to you. Don't trust anyone completely. Read the judge's order with great care to be sure it says what it was supposed to say.

If you discover, after the settlement decree has been issued, that something crucial has been omitted, it is sometimes possible to remedy the oversight by mutual agreement of the parties, followed by a court order. Only the court can amend its previous orders. However, if the parties cannot agree, the only recourse is further costly litigation—a contingency that argues strongly for making sure the decree is drawn properly in the first place.

Courtroom Behavior

We've all seen enough television shows to know what a courtroom is like. But, when you're there as a participant rather than a spectator, a courtroom is a cold, unfeeling, frightening place. Don't panic. Relax and carefully observe the rules of courtroom behavior. The decorum demanded by many judges makes Emily Post's rules of etiquette seem casual and undemanding. The magic words are "quiet," "propriety," and "composure."

"Quiet in the court," is the way the bailiffs say it, and woe be to those who fail to heed their warnings. A courtroom is no place for whispered chitchat. Those who indulge in it are out of order and may find themselves out of the courtroom. Quiet is required so that the judge, the court reporter, and the attorneys can hear every word of testimony.

You may be waiting for your case to be heard when you suddenly think of a question to ask your attorney. Ask him into the hall. If you don't, you may disturb the judge, which won't endear you to him when your own case comes up.

The Honorable Charles J. Fleck, presiding judge of the Domestic Relations Division of Cook County, Illinois, Circuit Court, says: "All lawyers must have integrity. Any statements made in open court directed to the bench must be honest. As an officer of the court, an attorney who purveys inexactitudes to the judge should be very severely dealt with by the court."

Be proper and cautious in manner and speech in court. Don't lose your temper. Don't call anyone a liar. Simply say his or her statement "is not according to the facts."

Four-letter words can spell disaster when blurted out in court. Consider the man who was appearing in a post-decree case. His ex-wife alleged he owed her five thousand dollars in back payments for child support. He was irate because he had paid her—but in cash, not by check, so he was without proof. Her allegations infuriated him because he was a good father, bought the children clothing and gifts, and visited them frequently. When his ex-wife's attorney charged him with arrearages at the hearing, the man shouted, "That's a God damn lie." The judge found him in contempt of court and jailed him for ten days. His language was a mistake, but the greater one was paying his wife in cash and not getting a receipt. When he lost his temper and used profanity, he also lost the opportunity for a fair hearing.

A belligerent attitude, loss of temper, and injudicious language can jeopardize your chances to win a judge's favor. As you are now aware, your opponents are trying to place you on the defensive. They're determined to make life miserable for you and force you to give up and give in. You should be smart enough to recognize their purpose and maintain your self-control. Prepare yourself mentally and emotionally for anything that could disturb or upset you in court. Keep your cool, no matter what. The judge will frown on emotional reactions, raised voices, and discourteous behavior. He may seize on your indiscretions as an excuse to rule in favor of your spouse. Don't give him the opportunity to decide the case on anything but its merits. Instead, give him cause to applaud your conduct. Let your spouse be the one who loses control.

It is also important to look the part as well as act it. Wear the proper attire. Dress is more casual these days, but don't wear your "in" clothes in the courtroom. Forget about the wild new plaid slacks or the fuchsia jumpsuit you bought for parties. You want to appear conservative, reliable, and self-assured. Dress more formally than you would for church. After all, a day in court *is* a day of judgment.

"I think that what you wear is very important," says one woman who is experienced in courtroom appearances. Men can deduce the male counterpart from her suggestions for women.

"It is true, of course, that how you act and the way you dress will depend somewhat on the individual preferences of the judge you will appear before, but it is difficult to know those preferences. You can't go wrong by being proper.

"If you think about it, your choice of attire should be self-explanatory. If you want to make a good impression, you won't go into a courtroom wearing a miniskirt. Although the judge would notice you and react to you as a woman, he won't react to you as a proper wife and mother, which is what you really want. If it is a custody battle, or you are trying to limit your husband's visitation privileges, the judge might wonder what kind of mother would come into the courtroom dressed like this.

"Age is also a factor. What you wear or how you do your hair will depend on how old you are. For instance, if you are forty-five, it would be inappropriate to have long, bleached blonde hair and a miniskirt. On the other hand, a twenty-one year old might get away with neatly combed long hair. I think makeup is all right, but it should be subdued. You're visiting a courtroom, not a nightclub.

"The point is that visual impressions help judges form judgments about character and personality. If your dress is inappropriate, the judge will question your judgment. If you are appropriately attired, the judge's first impression will be that you have good judgment, and are poised and mature; it will encourage him to believe what you have to say.

"Being properly dressed will also raise your own self-confidence. You will feel comfortable and confident, knowing your appearance is appropriate to the situation you are in."

Helen Schwartz, the lawyer who wrote the book *Lawyering*, feels that appropriate dress is important not only for witnesses but for attorneys as well.

"It's ridiculous that a woman should have to worry about what she wears in court," she says, "but I do feel I shouldn't be too flamboyant. I have a woman friend who wore a pant-suit in front of the Supreme Court. I don't think I could do that. I wouldn't risk alienating a judge, who has broad discretion in the courtroom. What I wear might hurt my client's case."

Making Your Points

At various times during your case, the judge will ask your

opinion about disputed issues. He may ask what you expect in settlement, whether or not you want custody of the children, or when you wish visitation rights.

Be prepared in advance for this confrontation. Prepare a succinct list of the items that are important to you. Don't try to read a prepared speech covering fourteen items. If you do, the judge will probably tell you abruptly and frankly that he has too many couples to divorce that day (and every day) to listen to an interminable "laundry" list.

Make your list short and your comments relevant or he'll ask you to come back in the afternoon to explain it to him when the courtroom is cleared. You don't want that to happen—it will double your fees to have both attorneys wait and appear later.

Instead, you should prepare a precise, short speech that will tell the judge what he needs to know about your desires. Strike deftly while you have the chance. If your list is too long, your opponent's attorney may stop you to ask questions and sidetrack you. If you want the judge to lean in your direction, emphasize the important issues and don't clutter your list of demands with insignificant, peripheral items or allegations. Make your point, but don't try to gild the lily or you may talk yourself out of a victory already won.

Testifying in Court

Your testimony on the witness stand can have a crucial affect on the outcome of your divorce. There are several techniques to keep in mind when you take your place in the witness box.

The first requirement, of course, is to tell the truth, for that is what you have sworn to do. But *how* you tell the truth also matters.

When your opponent's lawyer asks a question of you, don't answer quickly and thoughtlessly. Pause. Give yourself a chance to think, and your lawyer an opportunity to object to the question. You don't want to have already answered a question to which he may be raising an objection.

On the other hand, don't hesitate too long before answering

a question, either. The judge may get the impression that you are shifty and evasive. Taking too long to answer may suggest that you need time to fabricate a reply.

Testify only as to the facts, the things you actually saw, heard or know about, not what you believe. Do not draw conclusions. The judge will decide for himself how much weight or credence he will give your testimony. If the judge rules that something is immaterial, he'll tell you so. You will generally notice the judge penciling notations in his book, as questions and answers are elicited. It is your objective to be convincing. Hesitate just long enough before answering to indicate that your answer is thoughtful and accurate. Say "yes, sir" or "no, sir" in such a way that no one could doubt your sincerity. Your testimony must *sound* true as well as be true.

Word selection also is important for effective testimony. My earlier admonition to avoid absolute words applies in court, as well.

Words such as *every, none, always* and *never* seem innocuous enough until you or another witness testifies to some specific occurrence or event. Then, by adroit footwork, the opposition lawyers can destroy your credibility by proving the exception to one of those words. If you say you *always* took out the garbage or your husband *never* did, a lawyer will find times you didn't or he did. Inevitably, he'll make you look like a fool—if not a liar—and you'll lose points with the judge.

Remember, also, to qualify your statements with opinion words. Preface your replies with "I think," "I feel," "I believe." Qualify responses with words like *about, around, approximately, maybe, usually, generally, customarily*. When you use these as prefaces, you are hedging, and it will be more difficult to disprove your testimony or that of your witnesses. If, on the other hand, you are positive and dogmatic, you may trap yourself and, perhaps, antagonize the judge. You will be more convincing if you reply modestly and with restraint, and appear calm and rational.

As in the case of depositions, you may, during your testimony in court, feel the need to refresh your memory. Remember that old rule of law that says anything you hold in your hand while testifying can be taken from you by a lawyer, and may give him information you don't want him to have. You can avoid this by having another person hold your notes and documents for you while you are on the stand. If you need a specific document to answer a question, he or she can bring it to you, thus reducing the opportunity for the opposing counsel to gain information from you.

Scheduling Appearances

Most lawyers arrange courtroom appearances to fit their own schedules. Clients are commanded to appear at the designated time and place with little or no regard for their own convenience. A work schedule may be upset. A mother may have difficulty finding a babysitter. For many lawyers, that's the clients' problem, not theirs. If you complain, they will tell you it was the court's decision, not theirs. In fact, the courts give attorneys considerable latitude in determining when your case will be heard. The judge will look at his crowded calendar, the lawyers will check their pocket appointment books, and they will agree among themselves. Your desires won't be considered in most cases.

Make a point of having your needs respected, too. Don't sacrifice your own important engagements or jeopardize your job by remaining silent. Simply make it clear to your lawyer in advance that certain afternoons or special days are out of the question for court appearances. Most lawyers will note this on the outside folder of your case file and make appointments accordingly. Being insistent on convenient court dates is just one more sign that you are a fighter who will not be pushed around. Your attorney will probably respect you for it.

Continuances

At some point during your divorce proceedings, you will discover that your day of judgment is coming whether you are ready or not. It may be the judge or your attorney or your spouse's attorney who is determined to get your case over with now. You, however, may not be ready. For one reason or another, you may need time to consult with your attorney. If so, tell your lawyer you want him to request a continuance.

Continuances are court-ordered delays in the proceedings. Generally, a judge will grant them when either party, through his counsel, claims he is not ready. But more often, continuances result from the need to accommodate a lawyer or judge.

Some attorneys, eager to complete a case, will try to bluff their clients. They will try to convince them that a strict judge will refuse to grant any further continuances. The lawyer may actually refuse to approach the bench and ask for an additional continuance. If this happens, you have the right to approach the judge yourself and politely and respectfully request another delay. Usually the judge will grant it, especially if you need the time for further consultation with your attorney.

Willful Failure to Appear in Court

Should you capriciously not appear in court, as the judge instructed, it is possible he will find you in contempt of court. Your opponent may then be awarded the case on default. Your attorney should explain his strategy to you in regard to your court appearances or the lack of them at those times when the judge has not specifically required your presence. Be sure to inform your attorney if an unexpected business trip or personal emergency makes it impossible for you to appear so he can explain your absence to the judge. If you are absent without a convincing reason, you may be found in default because of failure to appear at the appointed time.

Missing Court Dates Because of Illness

Don't try to put one over on the court by feigning illness to avoid a court date. A suspicious judge will send a physician to your home or hospital room to find out if you actually are too ill to proceed. If the court-appointed physician decides you are a malingerer, the judge could hold you in contempt or grant a divorce to your spouse, by default. At the very least, you will have alienated the judge and likely prejudiced him against you. Genuine illness attested to by a physician usually will justify a continuance.

Setting the Trial Date

Fixing the date on which your case will come to trial often becomes a contest between the attorneys for each side.

Some attorneys push vigorously to secure an early court date. They press the opposition to name or agree to a "permanent trial date." However, if one is legitimately engaged in some other court or is otherwise unavailable when the date arrives, it may not be permanent even though you have papers stipulating that date. A presiding judge told me a date is permanent "if everybody's ready" and it is not permanent if they are not. One side or the other may press for a permanent trial date when they want to bring a halt to continuances and postponements. Or your own lawyer may press for a date if you have repeatedly delayed the case for frivolous reasons and he wants to conclude your case and get on to the next one.

Breathing Space

Maybe your case has reached a point where both you and your spouse are in the midst of serious negotiations. You want to avoid the expense of repeated court appearances and are not ready to arrange a date to go to trial. What you need is breathing space. You can save money on court costs and legal fees during this period by asking the judge to place your case on an inactive status. When you have everything worked out, you can have your case redocketed. Few attorneys inform their clients of this option because each court appearance increases their fees.

Lack of Notification

Occasionally, your lawyer may be unable to reach you to notify you of an upcoming court date. He may tell the judge that he was not able to reach you, but that he has your consent to proceed with the case. That may be an out-and-out lie, but some lawyers have done it. I know of instances in which a client was available almost constantly, but the case proceeded without his knowledge or consent.

Of course, an attorney representing you may indeed appear in court on your behalf without your prior knowledge or permission. He may be doing what he feels is right and best foı your interests.

But make him convince you this appearance was necessary. Protect yourself by keeping up to date and informed on scheduled court appearances. Have a clear understanding with your attorney on what he may agree to in your absence.

Ethical attorneys with the authority to appear for you in absentia are one thing, but, without this authority, they should never proceed. The attorney should postpone appearances until you are notified.

Courtroom Babysitters

What to do with preschool children while Mom and Dad are appearing in court is often a problem. They should *not* be dragged along to witness the trauma their parents are enduring or to disrupt the courtroom. Some courts have recognized the need for child care facilities and provide a playroom staffed by volunteers. Conciliation services may also offer babysitting services. Check in advance to see what facilities may be available to you. You may be able to eliminate the effort and time it takes to find a babysitter, as well as the expense.

Settling Out of Court

One of the tough choices that must be made during divorce proceedings is whether to settle out of court or to go to trial. Only about 3 percent of all divorce cases go to trial, largely because the legal expenses of a trial are higher than for out-of-court settlements. Often, however, trials can be worth the expense, particularly for husbands. Out-of-court settlements usually provide that the mother will have custody of the children, substantial provisions for their support and alimony or a large cash and property settlement. Hence, women tend to favor out-of-court settlement, where they can get the most by negotiation.

Most defendants will find themselves under heavy pressure to settle out of court. Be aware of the tactics judges and lawyers will use to pressure you when a trial is imminent. You must have a really strong case to continue to trial. And, even with a strong case, you probably will be urged to settle out of court. Lawyers from both sides and a coercive judge can be very persuasive.

Do not, under any circumstances, underestimate the coercive power of a judge. He has no desire to have a trial. He'd rather play golf or tennis. Besides, if he renders an incorrect verdict, you may appeal and his decision may be overturned. He'd rather avoid that risk by accepting terms established by the two opposing attorneys in a pre-trial, out-of-court settlement.

Your problem is imperative and immediate. You must have thought out in advance whether or not you want to settle out of court. You must be prepared. You must take care not to commit yourself before a judge to accept certain terms and conditions and lose bargaining points if the case goes to trial. You want the issues unsettled when you go to court.

So Settle Out of Court

Attorneys often try to save time and effort by settling out of court, particularly if a flat fee arrangement has been made. If your lawyer tells you, "That's as much as we can get . . .", don't accept his statement at face value. Most cases are settled out of court through negotiation. If you decide to take this route, you must be a crafty fighter. Follow your attorney through each step he takes so you understand and agree with the terms he's negotiating.

Don't try to rush the process. Hang in there until you get the provisions you want. Don't be railroaded into an unfair settlement because your lawyer says, "If you don't sign this by next week, we'll have to go to court." A court action may be expensive, but if it could give you a better deal than the one for which you are being pressured to settle, hold out for it.

Even if the negotiations seem to be headed in a satisfactory direction, be alert and skeptical. Don't settle for any verbal "gentlemen's agreement," because divorce court is not the natural habitat of gentlemen. Many oral representations may be made to you as an inducement to settle out of court. Most of them will be made privately, without the presence of witnesses. Any oral representation not verified in writing is virtually worthless. Judges and lawyers alike may deny that they ever made such a "ridiculous" statement to you in the judge's private chambers. And don't rely on your lawyer to back you up in any courtroom showdown over oral representations.

Another settlement trap to avoid is the "buy out." You can buy almost anything, for a price. Make sure the "buy out" is not a sellout by your attorney, or that it's not the judge who succumbs to temptations offered by your opponent's attorney. Make sure it isn't the witnesses who accept a little cash to testify against you.

If you do smell a rat, blow the whistle. Judges know that collusion and secret agreements are a way of life in this depressing field. Most of them really care, but they are swamped with thousands of cases each year. It's up to you to bring any suspected unethical conduct to their attention.

Acceptance of Terms

You may have a crafty negotiator and a tough fighter for your rights, but no matter how favorably you see the terms of your out-of-court settlement, they must be approved by the judge.

Once the judge takes over, he will decide if the terms and conditions agreed to are reasonable and fair to both parties. The judge, as I have stressed all along, has tremendous latitude and discretionary power in a case. Therefore, your object is to appear reasonable and sincere and not to arouse his ire.

At this point, the pressure on you increases. You must have the fortitude to stand behind the terms you have agreed to and to maintain the appearance of a reasonable person entitled to those terms. If you and your lawyer have set forth a fair set of conditions, the judge probably will grant you many or most of them. But if you insist on a long list of unreasonable, petulant demands, an irate judge may deny some that were reasonable and deserved. Concentrate on the major issues. Don't waste your energy or try the judge's patience with hair-splitting arguments.

Even if your demands ar reasonable, the pressure placed on you to give in may be unrelenting. Being prepared psychologically will enable you to stiffen your resistance and hold out until an equitable settlement agreement is reached.

Jury Trial or Not?

If either party asks for a jury trial, the request will be granted. If the choice is up to you, weigh your options carefully.

Generally, for men with substantial assets, a trial by jury is inadvisable. Juries are inclined to sympathize with the underdog in financial situations. That's why they extract outrageous settlements from "rich" insurance companies and that's why a sympathetic jury, picked by his opponents, will separate a wealthy husband from his property and assets. If you are a man, your spouse's lawyer will try to pick a jury of motherly women who feel that every woman should have her own home. After all, shouldn't the children be raised in comfort? When you get on the stand, the opposing lawyer will react with theatrical horror if you question the "right" of the mother to have the old family domicile. His carefully selected jury will probably share that reaction.

However, there are cases in which it may be advantageous to have a jury trial. For instance, if you intend to introduce evidence about your spouse's extramarital escapades or other amoral behavior, a sympathetic jury might well support your case. Your lawyer, of course, would try to select churchgoing, bible-reading jury members who would view your spouse's behavior unfavorably.

Discuss with your attorney the merits of requesting a jury trial in your case.

Discuss, also, the possibility of using an investigator-observer to assist in your case. Increasingly, large law firms are employing such individuals to assist them in appealing to the interests, attitudes and prejudices of members of the jury. The investigator-observer, once the jury is selected, carefully researches each of them. He learns all he can about their attitudes and the kinds of information and behavior to which they probably will favorably respond. In court, while the lawyers are talking, the trained investigator-observer is watching the reactions of each member of the jury. He then advises the attorney as to the kinds of behavior and testimony that appear to be influencing them.

Mistrials and Appeals

The conclusion of your trial, if you have one, may be only the first round of your appearances in court. Mistrials and appeals can prolong your case.

A mistrial may be declared for two basic reasons.

1. Some person prejudiced your trial so that you can no longer receive a fair hearing. Your attorney can then petition for a mistrial.
2. Attorneys for either side, or the judge, have made an error during the trial. A mistrial may not be granted automatically, but the judge may allow it.

Your attorney should know when to petition for a mistrial or a change of venue. Sometimes a judge declares a mistrial because he actually doesn't want to handle a particular case. It may be complex and require more of his time and energy than he wants to invest.

If, for any reason, a mistrial is declared, proceedings must begin all over again. This fact becomes a form of negotiating leverage for lawyers. The cost and delays of reassigning judges, and so forth, changes the momentum of a case.

To have grounds for appeal, careful foundations must be laid in the lower, or original, court. Only issues raised in the lower court and settled in the original decree may be appealed to a higher court. If you file a notice of appeal, it must be filed within thirty days of the lower court's decision. The appeal process itself, however, can take a year, and sometimes much longer. The cost of appealing a complicated case all the way to a state supreme court can run into the thousands of dollars.

10

Settlement Terms

THE "bottom line" in every divorce action is determined by the two spouses and their lawyers during settlement negotiations or, if they cannot reach agreement, by the court. The outcome will determine whether the divorce is a disaster for one or both parties or a solid foundation on which they can build more rewarding lives.

I have tried to stress, throughout this book, several basic objectives that should guide intelligent husbands and wives after they have decided to divorce:

1. Avoid a bitter court struggle over custody, property, alimony and child support. An equitable, negotiated settlement agreement will enable the parties to retain their assets, rather than to dissipate them on legal expenses.

2. Obtain a decree that is specific as to details and that anticipates potential future problems in order to make costly post-decree court actions unnecessary. This is also important for the emotional well-being of the couple, because their efforts to build new lives will be frustrated if divorce separates them physically but not emotionally and they continue the

same bitter disputes that have already destroyed their marriage.

3. Give priority to the welfare of the children, rather than to the emotional and psychological needs of the parents. The settlement and decree should provide adequately for child support and establish visitation privileges that will maintain a happy and reassuring continuing contact with both parents. Only thus can parents minimize the psychic scars that divorce inflicts on children.

Prepared, aware, alert and reasonable partners can avoid writing a tragic script for themselves and their children by striving diligently to reach a just settlement. A carefully drafted final decree will be specific and detailed. It will address itself to all of the circumstances that otherwise might renew the couple's battle in post-decree court. For example, a well-written decree will do more than grant visitation rights to the noncustodial parent. It will stipulate, as well, when that parent may visit the children, for how long, where they may be taken, and how and by whom they will be picked up.

The key to a final settlement that paves the way to a bright future is attention to details. A prudent spouse will fight to see that every contingency is covered. Don't assume your lawyer will do it. Too often, eager to collect their fees and move on to the next lucrative case, lawyers will not invest the time and effort needed to spell out clearly all the options available to their clients.

In previous chapters I have dealt with most of the fundamentals of custody, alimony, and property settlements. This chapter will acquaint you with some of the extras you might want to fight for in your settlement agreement and decree. The suggestions made here are not intended as a substitute for sound legal advice, but rather to alert you to what you can expect and may need to demand from your attorney. Discuss these ideas with him and weigh his advice thoughtfully before you try to incorporate them into your decree.

Custody and Visitation Rights

The financial aspects of divorce may provoke a vigorous contest, but for most parents, the determination of child custody and visitation privileges is the major battleground. If this debate is based on genuine concern for the best interests of the children—and is carried on outside their presence and without their involvement—it is probably healthy and can lead to a solution that meets their needs. If it is a spiteful contest in which the children are exploited to satisfy a desire for retaliation or vengeance, it is reprehensible and can only bring sorrow to all concerned.

No decent parent will willingly surrender contact with his offspring. Recently my young daughter replied, when I asked her if she knew I loved her, "Yes, 'cause you want to come visit us." Her answer made me stand ten feet tall. I gave her a big hug and kiss and told her that that was the nicest thing she had ever said to me.

Fathers, since they usually don't have temporary custody of their children while the divorce action is in progress, should be ready to state their visitation plans on their first day in divorce court. Determine when you want to visit your children (weekends, possibly some weekdays or holidays), because the judge will ask, and your attorney may not warn you that he will. From the first court appearance to the final settlement decree, noncustodial spouses must be prepared to spell out their desires for visitation and fight to win them. Otherwise, they may be reduced to begging, pleading, and arguing with a vindictive spouse in order to see their children.

Once the judge has made a temporary determination of visitation rights, the noncustodial parent should scrupulously take advantage of them. Children are easily disappointed, and they must not be made to feel that they have been abandoned. Each child must be reassured continuously that he still has the love of both parents.

The most important gift you can give your children when you visit them is a smile. Smile at them and mean it. A cheerful face, along with hugs and kisses, gives children a sense of stability and security. Let them know you're glad to be with them. Let tnem know you really love them. Show a lively interest in what they have done during your absence. Don't give them any reason to imagine that they are responsible for the differences that caused you to leave the family. If you are already separated, take the time now—with visits, telephone calls during the week, amusing notes and cards—to maintain rapport with your children and strengthen the parental bond so it can't be broken by divorce.

Visitation rights can sometimes be one of the most difficult and trying aspects of the divorce process. They often become an abrasive issue between husband and wife, and are therefore another source of argument and conflict that in turn affects the children. Both parents have an obligation to subordinate their own emotions to the welfare of their children by arranging and conducting visitations with diplomacy and maturity.

For the noncustodial parent, even more is at stake. If the judge has established adequate and satisfactory temporary visitation rights, and the noncustodial parent keeps his appointments faithfully and behaves in a manner that gives strength to the children, the odds are that the privileges will become permanent in the final decree. If, on the other hand, he demands visitation rights that he fails to use, or behaves improperly during visitation periods, there is every prospect that the presentation of these facts to the judge may result in a reduction of visitations in the final decree.

You will, of course, battle for detailed and specific visitation privileges in your final decree. One man I know gave his wife a divorce by default. She separated him from all of his assets and the final decree stated only in general terms that he was to have "reasonable" visits with his children. Now he must go to his ex-wife and negotiate each and every visit. His own carelessness and that of his lawyer in failing to specify his visitation rights has created an unnecessary problem for him and for his children.

While discussing visitations before the judge, try to convince him, through the reasonableness of your demands and the attitude you convey, that your primary concern is the welfare of the children, not your own. Avoid appearing excessively demanding, unfair, or uncompromising. It will help you to win his favor.

Visitation Smoothers

Provision should be made in your settlement decree to allow you or an agent to pick up the children for a visitation. Your agent could be any responsible relative or friend. I remember one father who had an automobile accident while en route to see his children on Christmas Day. He had a relative pick up the children because he couldn't get there in time himself. Had this agent not been provided for in the settlement decree, it might have meant a gloomy Christmas for the father and his children.

Another helpful stipulation is one permitting you to enter at any door of the house or apartment when picking up and delivering the children. Without it, and during inclement weather, a spiteful ex-wife could keep you waiting in the rain or snow.

Performance Bonds

Some uncooperative spouses manufacture excuses for failure to deliver the children at the agreed-upon time and place for a visit. One man I know, although he has remarried, drove seventy miles each weekend to see his children. Then, on two successive weekends, his ex-wife failed to bring the children to the store where he regularly picked them up. In an effort to enforce his rights, he held up her alimony check, only to find himself hauled into court for that offense and greeted by an unsympathetic judge.

His position would have been infinitely stronger if he had taken his wife to court. The custodial parent must show cause to deny a spouse visiting rights once they have been established by the court. If she doesn't, she is guilty of violating the court's orders. Similarly, a noncustodial parent must also scrupulously adhere to the visitation guidelines and the support requirements the court has established, or he can be found in contempt.

Instead of withholding the support payment, which irked the judge because it affected the children, my friend should have asked the court to require that his ex-wife post a performance bond to guarantee that his visitation rights would be respected. Performance bonds are issued to guarantee specific conditions. Violations lead to forfeiture of the bond amount. In the case of failure to live up to the requirements of the bond, the chances are good that the court will require forfeiture of the assets involved. Sometimes the judge will also order that custody of the children revert to the wronged spouse.

Most of these confrontations can be avoided by spelling out what is required of each party with respect to visits. Cover every contingency. Violations of the court orders are proved more easily if specific rights are defined in the decree.

Since parents often take their children on extended visits or vacations in a distant state or country, the noncustodial parent desiring to see the children is faced with a dilemma. He or she may be asked to send money for air fare for the children and a chaperon. If you were this parent, what could you do? It might be inconvenient for you to get the children yourself or to visit them at their vacation site. Some lawyers suggest you pay the fare and then deduct it from the next support payment. But if you do, you may end up in post-decree court. It is wiser to anticipate these problems by spelling out in the decree who will pay portal-to-portal travel arrangements, how often and so forth.

Most couples alternate visitation holidays. On Christmas and other special occasions, judges usually divide the children's day so they can see both sides of the family. When a custodial parent remarries and moves away, the court often provides that the noncustodial parent will have the children during Christmas week or longer and for an extensive number of weeks in the summer.

Remember that, at some time in the future, you may want to travel with the children to Europe or on some extended trip. These contingencies should be spelled out in advance so that, when such time comes, you don't eat up your vacation budget fighting for permission in court.

Your birthday should be your day with the children, many judges believe. Children's birthdays should be alternated or shared.

When it comes to conflicts with both parents wanting the same time slot, compassionate parents will do what is best for the children. Usually the problems of one parent will be more significant; or one parent may have seen the children a disproportionate amount of time so the other parent deserves his or her turn.

Young children usually have limited opportunities to visit their fathers, because most judges believe mothers to be better able to satisfy their needs. As children get older, judges often give the man more opportunity to be with them, even on overnights.

Many overnights for men occur on weekends from Friday night to Sunday night. Some parents, who have demonstrated they can't be trusted alone with a young child, may be required to provide a chaperon. Restrictions are sometimes set to minimize their opportunity to influence the child adversely, but this does not happen often.

The noncustodial parent should have the opportunity to arrange last-minute, impromptu visits. Maybe a long-lost relative stopped in for a few hours, or a friend couldn't use some tickets to an exciting game or event the children would enjoy. Provide for such spontaneity in the decree, or you probably won't have a chance to enjoy it.

If you request visitation during summer vacations, remember that the trend today is toward longer school terms. There is increasing consideration of a twelve-month school year. You may arrange a settlement believing that you will have the children all summer, only to discover that you will have them for only a few weeks. It may be desirable to try to alternate the times of year equally. Snowmobiling, skiing and similar winter sports are being enjoyed now more than ever before. There are Caribbean tours during the winters. The demands of your business may make some periods of the year more convenient than others. Remember, the four-day week is increasing, too. Short trips are more possible than ever before.

The prime thing to remember is that the needs of *the children should come first.* Any judge will express this to you, once he is convinced your marriage can't be salvaged. He will act to protect the welfare of the children and remind you that they are your responsibility. Any judge will want to make the transition easier for them..He will be more apt to grant your requests if you have shown that the welfare of the children is paramount in your mind. Prove to the judge you care for them, love them and show them affection.

Changes in Custody and Provisions.

Notification of Incapacity, Illness, Death of Custodial Parent

Many parents, in negotiating custody, overlook the possibility that something may happen to the custodial parent. Include a provision that, in case of death or incapacity, the other parent will be informed immediately. Also, try to include a stipulation that custody will revert temporarily or permanently to the noncustodial parent.

Odds are that the noncustodial parent would be named the custodial parent in any event. But, to avoid legal hassles with former in-laws, it is wise to protect yourself in case tragedy befalls your former spouse.

Looking toward the future, custodial parents who remarry should also realize that, in case of their death, their new spouse will have no legal obligation to care for their children unless he or she has adopted them. Occasionally, children may be thrown out in the street by a grieving and uncaring second spouse. While such behavior is rare, custodial parents should spell out some type of agreement with a second husband or wife about the custody and care of children in case of either partner's death.

Automatic Reversion Clause in Case of Desertion

An automatic reversion clause in case of desertion can also be valuable. One Illinois man discovered that his ex-wife had left their young children at home alone when one of them phoned and told him they were lonely and hungry and Mom was not around to feed them. They had missed school because they had been left alone. The father responded to the plea and retrieved the children. He then petitioned for custody, which the judge granted after a full day of court testimony. The judge wanted to determine the moral character of the father before he would allow him to have the children.

The stipulation that should be inserted, if possible, is one providing that if the custodial parent deserts the children, as in the above case, the other parent automatically becomes the custodial parent. Thus, without a court order, the children could come to the newly appointed custodial parent and stay with him or her thereafter.

Removal of Children by Custodial Parent

A man and woman divorce. The wife is granted custody of the young children, both parents remarry and a year or so later the ex-wife moves to a distant state. The children go with her and the father is separated from them by hundreds of miles. The decree assures him of visitation rights, but he did not anticipate the possibility that the wife might make it impossible for him to exercise them.

A mother with custody has sanction by petition to take the children anywhere she wishes. In the event of her remarriage or a career, given our highly mobile society, the above example is a real possibility. She may not attempt to petition the court immediately, and she may be unsuccessful the first time she does. But if she is persistent, she will petition the court again and again until she succeeds.

What can the father do to minimize this threat? He can attempt to write a provision of geographical propinquity into the final settlement. A man with a good lawyer and the will to fight to keep his family within convenient reach should be able to restrict a custodial parent's ability to leave the jurisdiction. In order to gain his approval, she would have to negotiate with him and grant considerations in return.

The traditional tragedy for fathers and children who love them is that, all too often, women have been allowed almost unlimited freedom to remove their children to distant locations. Children should have the right to see and be with their natural fathers. It is unfair to them, as well as to the fathers, to permit these unilateral moves without adequate consideration of visitation rights.

How can a father protect these rights? There are several ways. One is to fight for a stipulation providing that, if the children leave the area of close proximity to you, your support payments will stop or be greatly reduced. Such a stipulation gives your ex-wife a monetary incentive to stay.

Because the vast majority of cases are settled out of court, you do have leverage to negotiate or force safeguards such as this against your ex-wife's leaving the area. Should she refuse to accede during negotiations, you can insist you will go to trial. If your wife and her attorney are eager for an out-of-court settlement, they will be compelled to bargain. By yielding on other points that are important to your spouse, you may win stipulations guaranteeing that the children will reside near you. These should be nonappealable points.

However, even this agreement may not prevent your wife from petitioning the court at a later date. Her right to do so is expressed or implied with respect to written as well as oral agreements.

An example is a 1972 case in which the parties split and agreed the wife would get custody of the children. The judge agreed, despite an inclination to give the father custody because of the wife's unsavory past. However, the judge did allow a reserve without prejudice for the father to reopen the case and try for custody in the future. It was nip and tuck as to whether he or she would have obtained custody in a trial.

The father assumed that his spouse would remain nearby for a minimum number of years, as guaranteed by the wife, the attorneys, and the judge. Not so. Approximately thirty days after the settlement, he received a petition stating that his ex-wife had remarried and wanted to leave the area because her new husband had a chance to manage a firm in a faraway state. She asserted that it was in the best interests of the children to move.

The man now realized his mistake in settling out of court on terms that too readily allowed this implicit right to petition and leave with the children. Her implicit right includes changes in such circumstances as an ex-wife remarrying, a chance to get another job, a preferred climate, an opportunity to escape her reputation, a parent or relative who is sick and must be attended to, excessive living costs in the area or a desire to place the children in a better school.

The judge who had assured the father that he would not allow the ex-wife to leave the jurisdiction before the minimum years were up now told him, "Never in the state of Illinois has a woman ever been denied the right to leave the state if she has remarried. That is, if the new husband wants to leave."

Postscript: The ex-husband consulted the senior partner of his law firm and asked if there was anything he could do. His case had been settled out of court expressly because his ex-wife had agreed to remain in the area for so many years. The senior partner returned to the arena and had the judge look over the multitudinous papers and the record of the court appearances the couple had made. The judge changed his mind again. He stipulated that the ex-wife did, indeed, have to remain in the area for those years because it would be fraud to allow her to leave. This case is still in litigation.

The actual provisions you agree to in any negotiated out-of-court settlement must have the teeth to force an ex-spouse to remain in the area. The penalties and restrictions you put in the agreement are the clinchers.

What Are Provisions With Teeth?

Consider a provision that is enforceable the day a custodial wife leaves the area with the children. The provision would state that she and the children must meet with the ex-husband on a monthly basis to discuss the children's schooling, social progress, health problems and so forth. Travel expenses for the mother and children would be her responsibility. The meeting place would be designated by the father. An ex-wife would think twice before making a decision that would commit her to the expense and inconvenience of complying with such stipulations. Probably she would decide to stay in the area.

You can also protect yourself by fighting for a provision automatically reducing your alimony payments if a custodial parent leaves the jurisdiction. This doesn't restrict mobility, but the financial penalty may be sufficient to keep such a parent from leaving capriciously.

Consider another possibility. Have the custodial parent who decides to move far away pay you so much a month for the loss of your children's companionship and love.

Consider contributing to a special fund held in escrow for a ten- or fifteen-year period. The custodial parent forfeits the right to the fund if she or he and the children move out of the area.

Consider a provision that custody will revert to you if the custodial parent leaves the court's jurisdiction.

Try to insert a clause restricting your spouse from moving to any state that does not recognize your state in full faith and credit in regard to child custody cases. The judge should be able to tell you which states do. Such a clause may make it easier and cheaper for you to sue your ex-spouse and enforce decisions settled out of court. These states that do not honor your own state's full faith and credit would require you to hire another lawyer in the new state to which your ex-spouse has moved. This makes your chances of obtaining custody of your children or enforcing your out-of-court settlement decree difficult, if not impossible.

Anticipate in advance any possibility that your spouse and children might leave for a foreign country that does not recognize your state's full faith and credit clause in child custody. In the decree, restrict, if possible, their right to live in any such country.

If you suspect that your ex-spouse may move away for the deliberate purpose of separating you from your children, make it perfectly clear you would follow in order to be near them. Admittedly, few people could and would relocate in such a case. But, if you are sufficiently convincing, the threat that you will do so may deter the custodial parent from relocating to deny your children contact with you.

Prepare and fight. You may win.

Provision for the Children to Phone

It may seem a small item, but your children should be allowed telephone and mail communication with their noncustodial parent and other relatives. This is an important consideration, because a child needs all the contact with his absent parent he can get. Unless it is stipulated in the settlement decree, some bitter ex-spouses may not allow it. Put these terms in writing to make sure a vindictive mate will be in violation of a court order if she or he confiscates letters or denies the children their right to use the telephone.

School Information for Noncustodial Parents

Sometimes a custodial parent, intentionally or otherwise, will be most uncooperative about informing the noncustodial parent about the educational progress and problems of the children. Often it is an overt effort by the custodial parent to separate the children from the absent father or mother. For instance, a father may wish to attend special school functions that have significance for his children but be prevented from doing so because he is never informed in time. Or the noncustodial parent may be interested in the child's social progress as well as academic achievement and try to arrange a conference with the school principal or teacher. It may prove to be impossible because some schools refuse to cooperate without the expressed approval of the custodial parent. This denial of rights has the effect of degrading noncustodial parents to the status of outsider, even though their own flesh and blood are involved.

To avoid such emotional trauma, demand that your settlement agreement require the custodial parent to provide you with timely information regarding the children's activities and social and academic progress, and that you be given information about school activities far enough in advance that you can plan to attend.

Educational Decisions

In some states, a father with a college education is required to put his child through college if the child wants to go and would benefit from additional education. The child may not have seen or spoken with his father for years, but he is still expected to be an educational sugar daddy. This situation often results when the custodial parent assumes the right to make all the decisions without consulting the parent who is required to pay all the bills.

Make sure this doesn't happen to you by insisting on a stipulation that will give you equal rights in educational decisions. Stipulate that all decisions pertaining to the education of the children will be arrived at jointly. The children will benefit, because two heads are usually better than one. You will benefit, because you can exercise some control over educational expenses. A man required to pay for schooling without a voice in educational decisions is the victim of a situation akin to the taxation without representation that caused the Boston Tea Party.

If your spouse's attorney suggests a provision that you are to finance the children's schooling based on your "ability to pay," watch out. You may have a college degree but be earning very little when the child is ready for college. Based on your educational background, you still have the "ability" to earn, even though no one is presently paying you for that ability. Whether you are earning at capacity or not may make little difference to the court, and you could be held responsible for educational costs when you are without the means to meet them.

You can avoid this trap by demanding that your obligation to pay educational expenses be based upon your "means," rather than your "ability." This may get you off the hook if you are literally unable to afford the costs of an expensive college or university.

Children as Tax Deductions

Another source of perpetual post-decree conflict is the determination of which parent may claim the children as tax dependents. The fairer, more sensible resolution of this problem is to grant the deduction to the parent who is in the higher income tax bracket, since this yields the greatest tax savings. Often, however, a vindictive wife would prefer to save a few dollars herself, and give the rest to the Internal Revenue Service, rather than allow her ex-husband to benefit from the deductions.

If you and your spouse can agree at settlement time on this question, you can avoid many future disputes and problems. Many divorced couples have found themselves in deep trouble because both claimed the children as dependents. Several years later, the Internal Revenue Service has called them in to determine which parent actually was responsible for the support of the children. The spouse who could prove, through canceled checks and receipts, that he or she had provided more than half of their support was finally allowed the deduction. The other spouse was assessed additional taxes—and interest and penalties as well.

Situations like this, which involve legal expenses as well as interest charges and penalties, can be avoided by specifying in the original decree which parent will be allowed to claim the children as dependents. A provision of this sort is generally more important for the noncustodial parent—usually the father—who otherwise will have great difficulty in proving that he has, in fact, provided more than half of the children's support.

One option is to stipulate that the two parents divide the dependency deduction. This is eminently fair if both parents work and earn substantial incomes. Another is to provide that each partner share the children as dependents, one taking one or two and the other claiming the others as dependents. A third option is to alternate on a yearly basis in taking the deductions. However, this may not be advantageous if one parent has an unexpectedly higher income in a year when it is the other parent's turn to claim the deduction.

Perhaps the ideal solution for a father who is providing substantial child support payments is to persuade the mother to sign IRS Form 1220. This makes it possible for him to claim the children as dependents even if he hasn't contributed more than half of their support. The spouse who signs it is irrevocably stopped from claiming the children as dependents, even if he or she does supply more than fifty percent of their support in the future. Check with the Internal Revenue Service on this possibility, and clarify any questionable points with your attorney.

Obviously, this procedure is usually to the father's advantage, and most knowledgeable wives will resist signing the form. Thus, it may be necessary for the husband to make other concessions in order to obtain her signature. A man's decision to make some sacrifice in order to secure the right to claim the children as dependents may be influenced by a recent IRS ruling allowing divorced mothers with custody of the children to count the support their second husbands give them in determining whether or not they are responsible for more than half of the children's support. The father may be denied claiming the children as dependents, even though his ex-wife is unemployed and has no assets or income of her own.

Do a cost-benefit analysis of your own present situation and future prospects and determine what sacrifices you can afford to make to assure the continuing right to claim your children as dependents.

11

Negotiating to Win

IF you have paused in your reading to apply to your own situation the principles I have outlined, you may already have formed a reasonably clear concept of the settlement terms you will demand. Getting them will be another matter. You must now master the fine art of negotiation.

If you don't know it already, the judge or your lawyer will probably tell you that your case will rise or fall on its own merits. The fact that your friend Johnny Jones or Mary Brown got custody, the house, and a handsome property settlement is immaterial. Every case is different, and the outcome will depend upon how shrewd and convincing the parties are in settlement negotiations or in court.

Yet, it is important to know and understand the principles on which cases similar to yours were decided. If you are convinced that what you are demanding is right, reasonable, and proper, stick to your guns. Fight for your rights, but also look for leverage you can use to help you bargain more effectively.

Guardian Ad Litem

If controversies involving your children threaten to prolong your negotiations, consider the use of a guardian ad litem. This is a counsel appointed by the court whose sole responsibility is defending the interests of the children. If you are the more deserving parent, the use of such a counsel might help you gain custody of your children, or at least obtain better visitation terms than the opposition would otherwise be willing to concede.

Articles of Arbitration

Arbitration can be cheaper than court appearances and expensive lawyers. It usually is less traumatic than courtroom appearances, too. A time may come when your case reaches an impasse that must be resolved. Arbitration can provide a fair and just solution. Both parties agree to be bound by the decision of an arbitrating panel, which might be composed of a judge, a psychologist or sociologist and whatever other professional whose skills are appropriate. The panel should have an odd number of members so that a tie vote is impossible.

Work with Your Lawyer

In any agreement that must be negotiated, don't forget that your lawyer is your agent. If you have made a careful selection, he will represent your interests fairly and effectively. In some cases, though, the time may come when you conclude that you are not getting the quality of representation you need and deserve. If you find that your attorney is subverting your best interests and conspiring with the opposition, you will have to take the initiative. It won't be easy, because when you are up against the combined forces of both attorneys and perhaps the presiding judge, as well, the pressure may be enormous. It may take all of your courage and strength of character to resist accepting an unsatisfactory settlement out of court.

Make it clear to all parties that you won't settle for unfair or discriminatory terms. Make it perfectly clear to your lawyer that the longer the pressure continues, the less he is worth to you; the longer the delay, the more demanding your terms. Put the lawyers on notice that they can't drag their heels in order to run up larger legal fees, or pretend not to agree in order to prolong the emotional and financial trauma. In essence, if the other attorney and/or your spouse are being obstinate, causing you visitation problems, propagandizing your children or the like, make it clear you will fight them to the end, even if it means going to trial.

Developing Leverage

When the going gets tough, it's not only time for you to get going, it's also time to search for negotiating points you can use for leverage. One strategy, when making demands, is to offer alternatives. If, for instance, you ask for a change in the proposed visiting day with your children, ask for the day you want and a reasonable alternative. Given a choice of two days, the opposition is likely to concentrate on the choice between them, rather than on whether or not they want to let you change the day at all.

In negotiating, pick out the things that are most important to you. You're not going to win everything, so weigh the merits of each demand and be prepared to trade away the less important items. You may also fare better with the opposition if you show some compassion and understanding; often it will be reciprocated many times.

Fight for your rights on important matters, but don't be belligerent or arbitrary, and don't waste energy on nonessentials. Use them for trading stock to get what you really want. Take a lesson from labor negotiations: avoid forcing issues to the point where positions become so hardened that concessions can't be made by either side without loss of face. Concentrate, also, on understanding your opponents' bargaining techniques and strategies. Look for signs that tell you when they are bluffing, or others that reveal their strengths and weaknesses. Don't rely totally on your former ability to predict your spouse's reactions. She or he may react according to instructions from a lawyer, rather than as you expect on the basis of past experience.

Develop a sensitivity to the natural rhythms or plateaus in your case. There will be times when your spouse or his or her lawyer may be in a mood to get it over with and be willing to make some concessions to do so. This might occur in the pre-court stage, before a complaint has even been signed. Such a plateau may be revealed by attempts to intimidate you with innuendos like, "Surely you wouldn't want your behavior to become public knowledge?" or "You wouldn't want your children to know this, would you?" A plateau can also occur when you run out of money, or when you face the choice of an out-of-court settlement or a long trial. Be aware of these plateaus and try to use them to your advantage.

Your knowledge of your spouse's sins and indiscretions may also provide you with bargaining power. One woman, married to a self-employed man, was aware that he kept a dual set of books—one that reflected the true revenues of his business, another that he used in reporting income to the IRS. Although he had locked her out of their house, she was a determined fighter. She gained access by crawling through the kitchen window, got the books, had them copied, and then returned them. When they got into settlement negotiations, her husband and his attorney began to drive a hard bargain—until she revealed she had copies of the fraudulent books and threatened to turn them over to the revenue agents. Negotiations went her way after that.

Protect Yourself During Negotiations

You may find it helpful, as your negotiations proceed, to take a witness with you to bargaining sessions.

You should have confidence in your own ability to bargain and make correct decisions, but remember that you are so emotionally involved it is sometimes difficult to be objective. A knowledgeable and objective witness can monitor your lawyer's behavior and give you moral support. The witness may catch inferences or omissions that you, in a more subjective position, will overlook. Frequently, lawyers sense an impending settlement and omit, intentionally or unintentionally, terms that are desirable or even imperative for your future happiness and economic security, and that of your children. Your witness may detect these omissions.

Two heads are usually better than one, and the presence of

a witness may also help to keep the attorneys honest. Your witness can also help keep you alert to extravagant, probably unenforceable promises that are made solely to appease you, expedite a settlement, and enable the lawyers to collect their fees. It is far less likely that these tactics will succeed if you have a witness in your corner and both of you are prepared and aware when they are employed.

How to Win by Losing

Another lesson learned from labor negotiations—one that might have been used to save your marriage—can now be used to save your divorce.

If, in negotiations, you hold out for total victory, your opponents will go for broke. They have nothing to lose. But if you are sufficiently flexible that everyone can leave the bargaining table feeling like a winner despite forsaking some items that were crucial to them, all will have a vested interest in reaching and abiding by a settlement. You can't get everything you want. Once you have reached an agreement that is fair, reasonable, and proper, you and your spouse should have sense enough to bury the hatchet before the lawyers have confiscated all of your assets.

Beware of Oral Agreements

You now know that the wording of your final settlement decree is crucial to your future happiness. The writing of a good decree is an art practiced by few. If you're smart, you'll learn it.

There is no room in your settlement for oral agreements. Your decree should carefully spell everything out in writing. If at any point you are tempted to supplement it with separate oral agreements, remember the following case.

A Chicago friend of mine settled his divorce out of court on his wife's promise that she, a Catholic, would not marry again and that she would stay in the jurisdiction so he could see his daughter, then only four. He accepted her oral promise because it was a friendly divorce.

Eighteen months after the divorce, his ex-wife married a

man she was already living with. One week later she petitioned the court to leave the jurisdiction; her new husband now had gainful employment in a western state. Even though the decree specifically prohibited her leaving permanently with their child, the judge allowed it. The father tried every legal roadblock imaginable, but to no avail. The new husband chose a remote hamlet in which to practice his specialty—one where bus, plane, and train schedules made it virtually inaccessible to the father.

After the ex-wife moved West, she wrote her ex-husband that even though the Christmas visit agreed to in the post-decree petition allowed him first choice of days, she did not find it convenient to let him have his daughter for any days of the holiday period.

The father petitioned the Chicago court and was granted leave to go to this western state and pick up his daughter for the holidays. He arrived and was told his ex-wife had obtained a restraining order against him. Now he could not even see his daughter unless he was with her in the presence of the mother and her new husband, and then only in the child's own home and only upon twenty-four hours' advance notice. He learned the hard way that oral assurances are meaningless.

Put It in Writing

Spouses often say and do things in order to induce settlements and concessions but retain the unspoken option to change their minds.

You are a fool if you believe there is any security in an oral assurance or guarantee. The way to test the credibility of an oral assurance is to ask that it be put in writing. If it is a promise the other party intends to keep, there should be no objection. If there is an objection, you can assume it was not a promise your spouse intended to keep. You want a written settlement, with every detail thoroughly elaborated and carefully spelled out and every phrase interpreted and unambiguous. Insist on it before you affix your signature, no matter what you are told, even by the judge. Never sign anything with blanks remaining to be filled in. Never!

If, during the waning weeks of your marriage and the initial period of separation, you are subjected to continued harassment by your spouse, you may decide to incorporate even seemingly insignificant provisions into the decree to ensure that this treatment won't continue. If you do, make it clear to the judge that items that may seem petty to him are important to you because of the indignities to which you have been subjected by your spouse. If it seems necessary, describe some of the experiences that demonstrate the vindictive behavior of your spouse.

On some of these points, you may also have to convince your attorney that you are serious and intend to insist on details in order to reduce costs and trauma for you and your children in the future. Don't let him tell you that the other side won't sign the settlement agreement if it is as thick as a telephone directory. Convince him that *you* won't sign it unless it contains adequate guarantees of your future peace of mind, stability and security. Your attorney may be walking a tightrope between you and your spouse. He would like to make his job easier by persuading you to abandon some of your demands so he can get quick agreement from your spouse. Don't give in. Make him earn the fees he is demanding of you.

Vague language should also be avoided because it will not convey to post-decree judges the intentions of prior years. For instance, if you leave out provisions regarding college education, you may expect to be haled into court at some future date to litigate these items.

The attorneys, not the judge, draw up the settlement decree. You may win your case but lose it on settlement terms, if your lawyer lets his opponent write the settlement. Try to specify that your attorney, not the opposing one, will draw up the settlement terms. Interpretations often depend upon commas and wherefores, and you want these placed for your benefit, if possible. If some adverse understanding is omitted, so much the better. You're not playing tiddlywinks, and you want to grab every edge you can get. That, after all, is what the opposition is trying to do to you. The attorneys, of course, will have to cooperate on the final version until both are satisfied, but, if you are lucky, your opponent's lawyer may be careless.

Since timing is everything in any settlement, once a judge and the clients and lawyers have agreed to terms, they will hasten to draw up the papers to be signed within hours after agreement has been reached. Since they follow a standard form, it is not a difficult task. But, remember, even after you and your spouse and the judge have signed the document, there usually is a thirty-day grace period during which either party can rescind the agreement. A judge can also rescind it in protest and revoke it if it is a grossly unfair or illegal settlement. Just because it is signed doesn't mean it is final—until after the thirty-day waiting period.

Some less obvious details that will strengthen your decree are often overlooked. Some are of major importance and you should bargain for them from the start. Others you can bargain for as the opportunity arises along the way.

Sealing Charges

Often, because of bitterness, hatred or the need to allege grounds for divorce, sordid and malicious charges become part of the court record. Even though they remain unproven, they still become part of an official record open to the public that includes your children or anyone else who wants to read them.

As you near the end of your negotiations, when tempers have cooled, you and your mate may begin to regret some of the charges you have made against each other. If so, you should consider the merits of having the over-zealous charges withdrawn from the official court record or sealed for a set number of years.

You do have the right to try to insist that this be done; no expense is involved. Simply wait until negotiations near the end and then insist that a sealed envelope containing any damaging charges—proven or unproven—be held officially by the court. Put the burden on your attorneys to verify that all of the damaging materials are sealed, and require them to sign a notarized statement to that effect. Also, ask the lawyers for both sides to state in writing that they have no more copies of these charges in their possession.

Stipulating Legal Fees

A trump card a prudent and wary husband will want to include in any final settlement is a stipulation about the payment of his spouse's legal fees, both now and in the future. He must lay the groundwork for this item early in negotiations.

Suppose you've had an oral understanding during out-of-court negotiations as to your wife's lawyer's fees. Now the case has dragged on interminably and the bill is skyrocketing. It is time to play your trump.

Tell the judge you have steadfastly refused to sign any divorce settlement agreement unless it limits the wife's attorney fees to a specific sum that has already been agreed to, regardless of the number of appearances. On the basis of this information, the judge may order your opponent's lawyer to scale down his fees. Seldom will attorneys argue with a judge. They'll be before him again and do not want to risk alienating him and jeopardizing future decisions.

Early in the negotiations, try to force your opponents into committing themselves to a reasonable, set dollar figure for their legal fees, an amount you feel you can afford. Make sure this understanding covers all charges, regardless of the number of court appearances. Refuse to pay more. This action may reduce your costs and expedite your trial, for lawyers will not be eager to make appearances, knowing they will have difficulty getting paid for them.

Unless they are willing to fight to protect themselves, affluent husbands expose themselves to the possibility of horrendous fees for their wife's attorney, and often get little help from their own lawyer in resisting unfair charges. One man relates this experience.

"At one point in our negotiations, I discovered that my wife's lawyer was expecting a $100,000 fee from my wife. I, of course, was expected to pay. It was outrageous, but they knew I was well-off and her lawyer obviously was going to try to get what he thought the traffic could bear.

"I wasn't about to pay that kind of fee, and, in order to protect myself, I told my lawyer I wanted to bring the judge into the matter to decide what was fair. In fact, I told him I wanted to let the judge have something to say about the legal fees to be charged by my wife's lawyer, my own lawyer, and my trial lawyer. I said it in a nice way, but my matrimonial lawyer hit the ceiling and gave me the worst tongue-lashing I've ever received."

The experience wasn't pleasant, but, because he had the courage to fight to save his assets, the man learned from his lawyer's response that it wasn't only his wife's lawyer he had to worry about, but his own lawyers as well. Knowing this, he was able to appeal to the judge and to establish more reasonable fees for all three attorneys.

Generally in divorce cases lawyers try to get the exorbitant charge of ten percent of a man's estate; often a judge will allow it. This is a very good reason, as you were warned earlier, to dispose of as many of your assets as possible before engaging your attorneys. I would fight any attorney charging an unreasonably high percentage of my assets. The "rule of thumb" of ten percent is what lawyers *try* to get, but it's like the butcher's thumb on the scale: if you are watchful, you may not have to pay his price. Nowhere are fees so rigid that you cannot bargain, and if you can show that the lawyer was a prime cause of some of your difficulties, you may be able to drive an even harder bargain to get the fees scaled down or to arrange reasonable payment terms.

Most attorneys feel their job is done at the signing of the final decree. For your own protection, try to make stipulations regarding future legal fees part of your settlement. This is a two-edged sword. In general practice, a man has to pay the ex-wife's attorney for paper and courtroom work needed to enforce payment terms or conditions of the decree. In many states, the laws state that the man pays under these circumstances so a wife needs no such clause in the decree.

However, a man should stipulate that, in any future post-decree actions, he shall pay for his attorney and his ex-wife shall pay for hers. Or, stipulate that the plaintiff is to pay for his or her court costs. Psychologically, the future plaintiff may be deterred from suing if there is no carte blanche agreement that the defendant, or opponent, will pay for the legal fees.

If I were a woman, I would endeavor to include a stipulation that the ex-husband pay future legal costs necessitated by his actions. If I were a man, I would endeavor to avoid paying legal fees of a former spouse in actions brought to modify the decree for her own benefit. If one of the parties is better able to stand the financial costs, these stipulations may be impossible to attain. Then, too, the partner seeking the divorce may be in too weak a position to hold out for such concessions.

Attorney's Fees

The Honorable Charles J. Fleck, presiding judge of the Domestic Relations Division of Cook County, Illinois, Circuit Court, says: "My impression is that attorneys petition for fees in excess of what they will finally settle for in amount. Judges look to services rendered, whether it is a complicated case, assets involved, needless running up fees or costs, anything that will reduce the legal fees. The days are less prevalent where an attorney will be allowed just any fees by a judge. Judges act more independently today and will reduce legal fees given proper reasons to do so by the parties involved. In representing wealthy folks attorneys tend to do more work than is necessary, frequently taking needless depositions without even trying to settle the case first. I feel that many discovery motions are unnecessary. It merely runs up the fees to the people of means. It seems that if people have lived together for years, usually both parties have an awareness of each others assets. One would think it is a rare situation where one party secretes assets during the marriage. But with all the discovery and the purported reasons for it, you would think the reverse would be true."

One of the cleverest maneuvers I have observed in out-of-court settlements involved temporary fees. The wife's attorney had taken the case hastily, without checking her finances, believing that if the husband refused to pay, the judge would order him to do so. That is what it came to, and the wife's lawyer went before the judge to argue that he had contributed his time, ability, expertise, and experience, but had not been paid. He wanted the husband to pay.

The case was still in the hands of a pre-trial judge on an

unofficial basis. The husband responded that he didn't want to pay her attorney anything, but offered a token payment to mollify any anticipated opposition. He stated the amount he would pay and asked that his wife also be required to pay one cent. That, he said, was half of the fee because the lawyer wasn't worth two cents to her. The amused judge then ruled, "It isn't customary to stipulate legal fees in a decree. We will do it here. I can understand how you feel." He cut the fee the lawyer asked in half.

The wife's attorney was astounded, and more than a little miffed that the opposing counsel didn't help him. One lawyer seldom objects to another's fees. In this case, however, the man's attorney had kept records on a time basis and charged his client an hourly fee. The wife's attorney was trying to extract an exorbitant flat fee for the case. When he failed to get away with it, he sent a young, inexperienced member of the firm to represent the wife in subsequent negotiations.

Once you have convinced your wife's attorney that you will fight exorbitant fees, you will be on the road to a speedy and more favorable out-of-court settlement. Lawyers lose interest in prolonging the proceedings when there is no financial advantage in doing so.

Hopefully, the day will come when attorneys will collect fees from the person engaging their services and an adjustment will be made in settlement payments, depending on which party is held responsible for legal costs. There is already a trend in this more equitable direction. So fight for your rights. The more difficult you make it for attorneys to extort exorbitant legal fees from you, the sooner everyone will reach equitable settlements.

Another Way to Fight Exorbitant Legal Fees

Don't hesitate to protest to your attorney if you consider his fees too high. Begin by trying to negotiate a sum you consider fair under the circumstances. If the lawyer didn't do the job for you, deceived you or left many legal chores undone, complain. If you are able to reach an agreement for a sum less than the original demand, be sure to get it in writing and sent through the U.S. mails. That makes it official.

Should the attorney balk and assert that he has earned the higher fee, your last resort is to say, "Well then, sue me and we'll let the judge decide." Your lawyer knows full well that judges, to appear fair, often reduce legal fees, particularly if they are clearly outrageous. Judges dislike gougers, too. The threat may cause your attorney to yield.

Even if the judge decides against you, you can still appeal. You can ask the appellate court to consider an abuse of judge's discretionary power in awarding exorbitant legal fees. You can also appeal to the local bar association in protest of exorbitant fees.

Most of the lawyers I've interviewed have told me that, as a practice, they have never sued for payment of a protested legal fee, even if they believe the charges were justified. Lawyers don't want adverse publicity, nor do they want a client to call to a judge's attention their errors or oversights. Such actions can damage their legal reputation.

Some clients try to reduce charges without agreement by making what they consider a reasonable payment and marking the check "paid in full" on the back. If the attorney scratches it out and cashes it, the client will still be responsible. It also does no good to give the attorney a partial payment for services rendered without an agreement to that sum. It will be construed only as partial payment of an undetermined total.

Although the attorneys will pressure you to pay their bills in full and at once, you can bargain for more time to pay the bill, with or without interest, if your financial circumstances require it. Don't let them force you to put up collateral or charge unreasonable interest.

Many lawyers charge what the traffic will bear. One woman was approached by her lawyer, a member of a large firm in the Midwest, who asked her to pay an additional $10,000 after the divorce decree had been issued. She protested that he had already been adequately paid by her ex-husband, and indeed he had. The attorney remained insistent until she threatened to return to court to protest his demands. That was the end of the matter. Because the woman was a fighter, she won the round.

Jurisdiction in Future Litigation

In our mobile society, many people do not live all their lives in one state, and post-decree litigation can become tangled in the question of jurisdiction. As we've already seen, child custody cases can become derailed because an out-of-state court does not recognize, and will not enforce, the terms of a divorce settlement in another state.

Make an effort to safeguard the terms of your settlement by including this rider:

> This agreement shall be construed according to the laws of ________________. Jurisdiction shall remain with the Court of ________________ County in the present litigation.

Or try to include, as an irrevocable, nonappealable stipulation, that the original court will retain jurisdiction for post-decree litigation.

Kidnapping

The question of jurisdiction is often crucial because of repeated instances in which noncustodial parents have spirited children away to other states in order to escape the custodial determination of the court that originally granted their divorce. It is not uncommon for one parent to win child custody after a long court struggle, only to have his victory snatched from him by an out-of-state court that refuses to recognize the first court's decision.

A tragic consequence is the increasing number of cases in which parents are kidnapping their own children in order to obtain the custody that is legally theirs. In 1976, the newspapers reported the sensational kidnapping, in behalf of Seward Prosser Mellon, an heir to the Pittsburgh fortune, of his five- and seven-year-old daughters. The Pennsylvania courts had given Mellon custody of the children, but the New York Supreme Court awarded custody to their mother, Karen Boyd

Mellon. The unfortunate children became pawns in a seesaw kidnapping contest in which Mellon alleged that his wife first kidnapped the children in North Carolina. His agents then snatched them from a sidewalk in Brooklyn and removed them to Rolling Winds, the vast Mellon estate in Ligonier, Pennsylvania.

Kidnapping by parents has become so common that some detectives have become specialists in the field. One man in San Jose, California, Eugene Austin, has helped more than four hundred parents retrieve their children. He operates as a "parental agent" in behalf of parents who have legal custody, and who are willing to accompany him during the actual kidnapping.

The *Wall Street Journal* recorded an Austin "snatch" of the variety that has earned him the nickname "Mean Gene." The case involved a 22-year-old divorced St. Louis carpenter who had been granted custody of his three-year-old son after the child's mother fled to Florida with him in violation of an earlier court order.

Austin located the man's ex-wife and child and then asked the Miami police and the state's attorney's office for assistance in retrieving the boy. They advised him to have a Florida court endorse the Missouri court order and warned him not to break the law.

That was not new advice to Austin, nor did he receive it kindly. "The problem is that the militant guy with the guts gets his rights and his kids," Austin says. "The poor weak sister who doesn't want to fight and wants to do things legally gets treated like dirt."

Austin and the boy's father rented an apartment directly behind the one occupied by the wife and watched through the window until she appeared in the backyard with her son.

"Then we moved in to get him," Austin recalls. "We went up to her and tried to grab the child, and she started hollering for her boyfriend, who came charging out of the house with a baseball bat.

"We had to wrestle her to the ground and give her a light macing. I started to neutralize the boyfriend, but I saw he was going to hit a tree with the bat. Sure enough, he did—and he broke the bat, too."

With the boy in their custody, the two men hurried to their rental car, drove to a nearby shopping center where they had parked a second rental car, and began a circuitous 1,300-mile trip back to Missouri, staying at a succession of safe houses that are provided by an underground of divorced men who help each other in these situations.

A more typical case is that of an Illinois father who was granted custody of his daughter, only to have his ex-wife remove her to New Jersey. He appealed to a lower court in New Jersey, but the judge refused to honor the Illinois custody decision and insisted on rehearing the entire case, a court action which had already cost the father about $20,000.

Rather than endure this expense again, the father appealed directly to the New Jersey Supreme Court to order the lower court to honor the Illinois decree. The supreme court refused to hear the case. The distraught father, who was desperately concerned about the welfare of his daughter while in the custody of her mother, was now confronted with a bitter choice. He could go through another trial in New Jersey, at considerable expense, but this would involve a lengthly delay during which the child would remain with her mother. The second alternative was kidnapping, and that is the one he chose.

The father enlisted the help of a friend who flew with him to the New Jersey city in which his wife and daughter were living. Each man was armed with a duplicate original of the Illinois custody decree. On arrival in New Jersey, they rented a car and located the wife's residence, which was only a block from the New York state line. They then checked on the location of the daughter's school and made several practice runs over the route the school bus followed, to check its timing. Finally, they drove to the corner where the daughter was waiting for the school bus. The father leaped from the car, grabbed the girl—her school books flew into the air—and dragged her into the car. They then sped across the state line into New York and followed a zigzag route to an airport in Connecticut.

Within forty-five minutes, the New Jersey State Police had put a kidnapping alert into effect. By then the father and daughter were already safely out of that state's jurisdiction. However, the child, who had been thoroughly propagandized by her mother, was extremely angry. When they arrived at the air terminal in Connecticut, she screamed at her father and called him every ugly name imaginable, arousing the attention of airport officials. They were aware of the kidnapping alert, identified him from the description and took him and his friend into custody. But because he was able to show the duplicate original of the Illinois court order, establishing that this was clearly a domestic dispute, and because he was not in defiance of any Connecticut court order, officials escorted the father, daughter and friend to the airplane and permitted them to return to Illinois.

Although the daughter has since adjusted well to life with her father in Illinois, the emotional and psychological impact of her experience certainly was not in the best interests of the child. Yet, for a parent with legal custody who was concerned about the environment provided by the mother, what else was there to do?

Anything you can do to obtain a decree that will make this sort of action unnecessary in your case is worth whatever effort and sacrifice it may require.

Finalizing the Decree

Mutual Releases from Liability

Once you and your spouse have agreed to end your warfare, try to make sure the hatchet stays buried. To assure yourself that you won't be back in court, hamstrung by an ancillary lawsuit, write a mutual release from liability into your final decree.

If you have evidence of unethical conduct on the part of the attorney, giving grounds for a malicious prosecution suit, breach of ethics case or the like, you may use it to win other points in exchange for a mutual release from liability. You can still settle out of court and release the lawyer from legal liability, but you retain the right to protest his conduct to the local bar association.

Enforceability

You can also protect your future interests by bargaining for a nonappealable decree. If you have achieved the terms you want in the original decree, this clause will preserve your victories in the future.

Records

Even if you've won the terms you hoped for, it may become a hollow victory if your spouse violates the agreement. If you suspect that this may happen, you can prepare yourself for the post-decree litigation by engaging your own stenographer to record the court proceedings. The presence of your personal court reporter may act as a psychological deterrent that warns your opponents that you intend to go to court to enforce the decree. Your private stenographer may be more reliable than the court's official reporter in the event you proceed to higher courts. The cost will be yours, but you will have more accurate records at your disposal that may be crucial in any trials or appeals. It is not unusual for official records to be lost or destroyed, whether by accident or design. If you have your own transcript, you are protected.

Swearing to Terms

After you have agreed upon the terms, consider having your attorney ask your spouse, under oath, to take the witness stand and swear, declare, and affirm to you an agreement to abide by each and every item in the settlement agreement. Make this affirmation of the terms in court a pre-condition to your signing the final decree. The signing occurs after these sworn agreements and assurances, not before.

This act will strengthen your case in the event of post-decree violations. If your spouse refuses to make such a declaration under oath, you have your warning. He or she probably doesn't intend to live up to the terms of the agreement.

Signing Settlement Terms

Read carefully and thoroughly every word in the settlement document, to be sure you fully comprehend its meaning. If any point is unclear or ambiguous, ask for an interpretation and have it spelled out more clearly. Your life and your divorce are at stake, so don't leave all the responsibility to your attorney. Even if he's good, he isn't Superman.

If your opponent's lawyer insists on writing up the agreement terms for your lawyer to look over, be doubly cautious. Look for omissions, deletions, and changes injurious to your interests. Question every word and phrase until the meaning is crystal clear.

Be prepared for the eager attorneys and judges who breathe down your neck with pen in hand, insisting you sign an agreement you have only hastily read. Be prepared for assurances that "It's what was agreed upon," "It's a good deal" or "Quick, before he changes his mind."

Women should be particularly wary of one of the common ploys of attorneys who are eager for a settlement. Hear it from a woman who experienced it.

> It seems to be a standard line on the part of your attorney, when he is pressuring you to finalize the divorce agreement, to use the point that "You are such an attractive woman that you are bound to be remarried in two years. Why in the world are you so worried and concerned about your financial security in the future?" It's just a standard, gimmicky line they all use. I'm not the only one. I know half a dozen women who have laughed hysterically about how attractive they are and signed on the spot without thinking about the consequences.

The attractive woman who recounted the experience was divorced nine years ago. She's still unmarried.

Remind yourself that lawyers are experts at paraphrase-itis. That is their business. You can afford to wait long enough to study the document carefully. Sleep on it. It's your future, not theirs.

Before signing, insist that there be enough copies available so you can have a *duplicate original* before you walk out of the room.

In the shady divorce field, how can you possibly tell who is honest? After sitting through more divorce cases than I can count, I can't. Dishonest lawyers and officials can add paragraphs, change meanings, add words. Strange new clauses, labeled "understood and agreed to and initialed by the parties," pop up all too often, to the chagrin of couples who never agreed to any such thing. The lawyers have the official copy and, unless you have a duplicate original, you cannot dispute that you signed it. By insisting upon having a duplicate original, you will eliminate or reduce the possibility that a contract altered in your opponent's favor will be recorded by the judge. The lawyers may not want you to have one, but insist. Do not sign without it. This is the time to trust no one but yourself.

Enforcing Your Decree

You eliminate a lot of disputes and legal fees if you remember that anything legal and stipulated in a decree will be ultimately "enforceable" in the post-decree courts or even the state supreme court, if it comes to that. Oral agreements are not. Once you get this distinction firmly in mind, you can approach your settlement negotiations with judgment and determination.

Post-Decree Considerations

In many cases, the divorce decree is not the end of litigation but the beginning. Too often, items not spelled out in the divorce decree become the subject of post-decree court appearances.

Some evidence you may have against your ex-spouse may not have been brought out in an out-of-court settlement. Some lawyers tell their clients that this becomes moot after the signing of the decree, and new evidence will have to be developed from post-decree behavior in order to petition for changes in settlement terms.

Often, in post-decree suits over child custody, astute parents have accumulated information, witnesses, and data they would like to introduce. Everything that applies to the welfare of the children, whether it occurred before or after the decree, is admissible in post-decree hearings. Thus, any actions or events that had bearing on the child's welfare can be reserved as future evidence.

One of the most significant opportunities a man or woman has in post-decree litigation was suggested by a senior law partner of a prominent firm. He urged that a male client who wants custody make an appointment with his attorney after his case is concluded. He should ask the attorney to tell him exactly what to do in order to obtain custody. The advice will be to document harassment, restrictions on visitations, neglect or abuse of the children and the like. The noncustodial parent will be told to identify witnesses and be able to cite specific incidents and the dates, places and circumstances in which they occurred.

Sometimes it is also possible to collect the statements of the children themselves. They may openly declare their desire to reside with you permanently. They may testify against your spouse, in this case, to corroborate her or his neglect or abuse, or statements she or he has made to them propagandizing against you. For those dads or moms who are determined to win custody, and clearly deserve to win, victory is often easier in post-decree court than in the initial divorce action.

A short conference with your lawyer to discuss post-decree suits may give you the information you need to enforce settlement terms, change custody or modify settlement decrees. I recommend it, especially for people who desire custody in the future so they will know exactly what steps to take and how and when to take them.

Finally, let me restate the fundamental principle that nothing is settled until it is settled right. You will always fare better with an equitable settlement—one in which you neither won too much nor lost too little. An unfair settlement will prove to be a hollow and transitory victory. It will return to haunt you.

12

Hope for the Future

EVEN in amicable, uncontested situations, divorce can be a gut-wrenching experience. And the trauma rarely ends with the decree. Despite the frequency of divorce, a stigma still is attached to it, at least in the minds of the divorced couple, who cannot escape feeling that the divorce was somehow proof of their own failure.

Single again, many divorced persons who could scarcely wait for the day their marriage would be over find their new freedom less invigorating than they had hoped. Close friendships they had formed during their marriage seem to have dissolved. Relationships with favorite in-laws are severed or strained. Familiar, comfortable routines are broken. The new apartment, despite the care put into it without the need to consider the wishes of another, is sterile and empty because there is no one to share it with. Even sharing your bed with a different partner every night becomes old hat when you have the freedom to do it.

Husbands miss the convenience of a well-run household, or even the inconvenience of the disorderly one they were accustomed to. They mourn the loss of daily contact with their children. They soon tire of restaurants and quickly learn to hate their own cooking and the solitude in which they consume it.

Wives still trapped by their household chores and children resent the freedom they believe their ex-husbands are enjoying. The dinner hour arrives and they long for respite from the kids and the opportunity for adult conversation. Their trials and tribulations loom larger because they have no adult sounding board for their complaints. The screen door parts from its hinges and suddenly there is no one to fix it. The phone that once rang to produce friendly invitations from other couples hangs mute on the kitchen wall.

The post-decree months for many divorced men and women has been described as a "period of mourning." For many it is precisely that, but it need not be. Rather, it should be a period of rebirth during which a new life rises from the ashes of a dead marriage. It is a time when both parties—husband and wife—must make a choice. They can pull themselves together and carefully structure a happier existence—or wallow forever in frustration, self-pity and despair.

For couples with children, the quality of the life that lies ahead may be determined by their ability to put past differences behind them. Visitation arrangements make continuing contact between the divorced couple almost inevitable. If each of these encounters brings forth a renewal of past disputes, their future will stagger under the weight of a dead romance. How much better for all concerned, particularly the children, if the parents vow to provide their offspring with what they have always deserved: an opportunity to enjoy the love and affectionate guidance of both parents in an atmosphere from which all recrimination and tension have been removed.

Life after divorce actually can be rewarding for both parents, and certainly for the children. Dads will find that their relationship with their children, concentrated in relatively short visitation periods, becomes more intense and satisfying to them, and more meaningful for their sons and daughters. Many noncustodial fathers have told me that their relationship with the children was never as close during their marriage. Custodial mothers, meanwhile, relieved of responsibility for their children during regularly scheduled visitation periods, suddenly find that they can plan new activities and develop new interests that previously were out of reach. The children blossom because tension and uncertainty is removed from their lives and, although they receive it separately, the combined attention given them by their mother and father surpasses anything they experienced when the parents were together.

In time, most divorced men and women will consider remarriage. Typically, unless they are victims of the "rebound" syndrome, they will choose their second mates with extraordinary care. Having experienced the agony of one divorce, they don't want to risk another. "I wouldn't go through another divorce for a million dollars after taxes," said one of my friends. I know how he feels.

Not surprisingly, a second marriage is often more successful than the first, particularly if both of the partners have been divorced. The sense of failure that accompanies a divorce prompts most victims to consider carefully the shortcomings that destroyed their once happy romance. Armed with this knowledge, they are better prepared in the second marriage for the give-and-take that is essential to a happy and enduring relationship. Often, too, couples who have children in a second marriage find that they are much better equipped for parenting. They have already had some experience and can profit from their mistakes. They have learned in custody negotiations how much their first children really mean to them. Finally, because they are older, they are less inclined to regard their children as a burden that interferes with the social activities many younger couples would like to pursue.

So don't feel hopeless about your future. There is another rewarding life for you if you work for it, and perhaps even a happy second marriage. One evening, I interrupted my work on this chapter to attend a meeting of a singles group: unmarried, divorced, divorcing, and separated adults. It was the first anniversary of the group, which was formed to give singles an opportunity to meet and enjoy each other and to discuss common problems.

Among those present at the affair were a pair of newlyweds

who had first met in the group. During the evening, they expressed their gratitude to their friends and thanked them for the Bible they had received as a wedding gift. When some of the women applauded the handsome new husband, he blushed and asked them why they did it. One of the women quickly replied, a smile on her face and in her voice: "Because you represent to us the hope for the future. If Ann can get married again, then there is hope that we may, too." It was because of such a happy occasion that I chose this title for this chapter.

I remember, in the darkest moments during and immediately after my own divorce, friends and relatives who counseled me, "This, too, shall pass." I scoffed because I thought there would never be an end to the litigation and to the emotional strains that accompanied it. But there was. I can now say to divorcing men and women, based on firsthand experience, "This, too, shall pass." Adjustment won't be easy, and there will be many pitfalls ahead, but you may avoid most of them by sharing the experience of others.

If you read the women's magazines or watch the tube, it may appear that singles have all the fun. The swinging life. Mod apartments. Flashy clothes. A date every night with the man or woman who invaded your dreams in the dying months of your marriage.

Don't believe it. Most divorced men and women find that the single life isn't remotely as glamorous as its media image promises.

Many ex-wives complain that dating bears no resemblance to the happy evenings they enjoyed when they were sweet sixteen. Their male partners too often have a chauvinistic hang-up stemming from the obvious fact that a divorced woman has long since parted with her virginity and from the presumption that she has sexual needs they are eminently qualified to fulfill. Listen to this woman.

> During my marriage, my husband and I had a close relationship with two other couples. The men had gone to school together and remained firm friends after they got married. My ex-husband was an alcoholic, which was the primary cause of our divorce, and for a year and a half after our separation we con

tinued to see each other, hoping he could work out his problems and remarry. Then, suddenly, he died.

Almost immediately, his two school friends—both of them still married to women who were close friends of mine—began making advances. I would get calls suggesting that, since they had the afternoon off, we could go someplace where we can be a little more friendly. A couple of times they proposed directly that we go to a motel. This scared me so much that I didn't date for a long time.

Finally, after many invitations, I dated a man I met in a singles group. On the third date he asked me to marry him. I thought it was a bit premature and mentioned it to a girlfriend who belonged to the same singles group. I discovered that the man had dated other girls in the group—one in July, one in August, another at Christmas time—and in each instance had proposed to them on the third date.

The pattern was incredible, and more so because none of the girls he proposed to appeared to have anything in common. Why was he attracted to us? We finally figured it out. We all owned our own homes!"

Like these women, many ex-wives complain that too many of their dates have instant sexual expectations and are hard to convince that it isn't the paws that refreshes. There are other problems, too. One divorcee said, "Remember to tell your readers to date 'ex-' instead of 'x-rated' dates." Many of the men she thought were single or divorced were simply cheating on their wives.

One divorcee dated a man five times before she discovered she knew his little boy. His face turned white when she told him that she was a teacher who had his son in her class at school.

Divorced parents also may find that dating is less convenient than in their pre-marital years. Continuing responsibilities to care for or exercise visiting rights with children often interfere with their social freedom. It isn't always easy for a man to find a young woman who will be thrilled to spend every Saturday night with his children, attending a baseball game or reading them stories. The children themselves may make relationships difficult, if they are resentful of the new man or woman in your life and unable to accept the prospect that you may remarry.

But remember, your first marriage wasn't easy, your divorce wasn't easy, and there is no reason to expect that rebuilding your life will be easy, either. If you are determined, resourceful and wary, you can find happiness. Here is the other side of the coin, from a divorced woman who has made a superb adjustment and is now living a rewarding existence.

> I think that people should be extremely leery of getting involved with someone else immediately after their divorce. Statistics show that when divorced men and women remarry before a year has passed, they often repeat their first experience. Nevertheless, however bad a time they had in their first marriage and divorce, they shouldn't let it spoil their future relationships. They shouldn't become paranoid and cynical. If they do, it will destroy any chance for happiness they have.
>
> On the other hand, I don't feel that there's any crime in not remarrying. I don't think marriage is the answer to everything. Happiness first must be found within yourself. Divorced persons should devote much of their time to the children, helping them to adjust, because children have so many adjustments to make. They should also work on those things within themselves that they feel contributed to their marital problems, or try to improve aspects of their character and personality that they feel are lacking. This is a good self-assessment, self-improvement, self-enrichment time.
>
> Learn to know yourself. Learn to understand yourself. Learn the good and bad aspects of your own character so you can be accepting of them and be comfortable with yourself. Once you have become open and honest with yourself, you can allow yourself to be accepting of another struggling human being. This is necessary before you can have a successful, in-depth relationship.
>
> Only after people have gone through this process and are at the point they feel they understand themselves better should they begin to think about developing serious personal relationships with persons of the opposite sex. That doesn't mean they shouldn't participate in groups or get to know people in the period immediately after divorce. They *should* use some of their time to make friends and get back into the mainstream, but getting seriously involved with one individual is, I think, a bad mistake.

> When they reach the point where they decide they do want to marry, they should carefully think through the reasons that are motivating them. Have they found a person they would want to be with for the rest of their lives; who they feel will make them far happier than they are now? Or are they contemplating marriage simply to find a mother or father for their children, or to gain greater financial security? I believe people must examine their motives with great care if they are to avoid making the same mistakes they did before.
>
> If, after this kind of self-analysis, they are still determined to remarry, they should then review carefully their first marriage, identifying why it went wrong and the aspects of their own behavior that contributed to the divorce. They should resolve to make a conscious effort not to repeat the errors, and to overcome the shortcomings, that created problems before.
>
> What kind of a person would I look for? I would look for someone I could trust, someone who will give me a sense of security, someone who will be genuinely concerned about my children, someone I can enjoy being with and who shares my interests. I think financial security is also an important consideration, not because I am mercenary, but because the financial commitments that stem from divorce put a horrible burden on many second marriages and may become the rock on which they founder.

Financial problems often abound in second marriages. One never has enough money. But there are many other adjustments to be made in a new marriage, particularly emotional adjustments. These problems are perhaps more important than financial difficulties. Try to understand why your first marriage failed and consider preventing a second failure through extensive premarital counseling. Until now, you have probably blamed your spouse for the failure of your first marriage. You owe it to yourself to be more objective and to honestly assess the extent to which you also contributed to that failure. Premarital counseling also may help you make sure you and your prospective spouse really do know each other and are aware of each other's shortcomings. Love need not be blind.

If you do decide to remarry, disclose fully to your intended the extent to which your shortcomings contributed to your divorce. Show your bride- or groom-to-be a copy of your divorce decree. She or he has a right to know what restrictions your divorce settlement may place upon your future.

A second mate, for example, can become contingently liable for the spouse's obligations under the decree. It's only fair to reveal these commitments in advance.

A man should be made aware that his future spouse, if she is the custodial mother, is limited to a geographical area for a specific time period so he will be prepared to adjust his plans accordingly. A woman's marriage may be shattered if her new husband has not been told and is forced to choose between his marriage and a more exciting and lucrative job elsewhere. If both parties are familiar with the details of their intended partner's first marriage, they will have greater insight into how each has reacted to stress in the past and may better be able to avoid behavior that may duplicate it in the new marriage.

You should also consider assuring the success of your new marriage by entering into a premarital agreement. Couples frightened by divorce statistics or scarred by their own previous divorces have realized the wisdom of spelling out their marriage contract in legal as well as religious terms, and more of these agreements are being written every year.

Such agreements should state what is expected of each mate. Property owned before marriage by each spouse should not be commingled and should subsequently revert back to that spouse if they part company. A formula should be agreed to, in advance, as to child support and alimony.

What about inheritance? Maybe you wish to see your children first in line for inheritance rather than your new spouse. Perhaps you want to see your pre-marriage stock portfolio go to your children for their protection and education instead of to your new spouse's children. These conditions should be discussed with and understood by your spouse and spelled out in the agreement.

A prenuptial agreement does not indicate a lack of confidence. On the contrary, it can be a positive, constructive, creative and thoughtful document. It should be fair to both sides. It can protect both parties from the liabilities of former marriages and, in case of another marital failure, it can make divorce a relatively simple and inexpensive process. It has the salutary effect of reducing a future attorney to the status of errand boy. His gigantic fees will be greatly reduced if there is no property or custody to fight over.

A prenuptial agreement should be considered by almost anyone contemplating marriage, even for the first time. Most of the things divorcing couples fight about can be determined in advance in such agreements. A nonappealable, enforceable, nonnegotiable prenuptial agreement with teeth may provide us all with the vehicle that has long been so elusive and so much needed in this grubby field of divorce. If it is fair to both parties and spells out terms and conditions and procedures, what could be better?

Prenuptial agreements alert the couple to their marital responsibilities and provide some pre-marriage education. Rather than take the romance out of a marriage, they can eliminate causes for argument and free more time for romance. For a couple in love, such an agreement may seem like a crass, pragmatic exercise, but what can it really cost, compared to an expensive, traumatic, heartrending divorce? The time to agree to rational terms is while people are in love and anticipate no divorce at all.

Concentrate on yourself after the divorce, and on your children. Don't worry, fret or fuss about what your ex-partner is or is not going to do. Concentrate on your own life and your own household or, if you are a noncustodial parent, on creating a home environment that your children will love to visit. By being positive and constructive, your opportunities to meet new friends and to enjoy life once again will be much greater than if you remain consumed with hatred and bitterness toward your ex-mate.

Finally, although you deserve happiness for yourself, you

owe it to your children. Noncustodial parents, particularly, should consider carefully what they can do to minimize the emotional damage inflicted on their children.

Guidelines for Life During (and After) Divorce

The Cook County, Illinois, Circuit Court's Divorce Division distributes guidelines for visitation that contain good advice for divorcing parents in any court jurisdiction. They are reprinted here by permission.

> You are involved in a divorce suit and are the parents of minor children. Children are usually the losers when their parents separate. They are deprived of the full-time, proper guidance that two parents can give—guidance and direction essential to their moral and spiritual welfare.
>
> Although there is probably some bitterness between you, it should not be inflicted upon your children. In every child's mind there should be an image of two good parents. Your influence with your children will be helpful if you will follow these suggestions:
>
> 1. Do not poison your child's mind against his or her father or mother by discussing shortcomings. Do not attempt to buy your child's favor by presents or special treatment.
> 2. Do not expose your children to any member of the opposite sex with whom you may be emotionally involved (before the divorce).
> 3. Do not use your visitation as an excuse to continue arguments with your spouse.
> 4. Do not visit your children if you have been drinking. Do not visit your children at unreasonable hours.
> 5. Be prompt in paying child support as ordered *in cash*. You will not be credited with presents, clothes, etc., as part of the child support ordered.
> 6. Do not fail to notify your spouse as soon as possible if you are unable to keep your visitation. It's unfair to your children to keep them waiting—and worse to disappoint them by not coming at all.
> 7. Make your visitation as pleasant as possible for your children by *not* questioning them regarding the activities of your

spouse and by *not* making extravagant promises you know you cannot or will not keep.

8. The parent with whom the children lives must prepare them both physically and emotionally for the visit. The children should be available at the time mutually agreed upon.

9. If one parent has plans for the children that conflict with the visitation and these plans are in the best interests of the children, be adults and work out the problem together.

10. Always work for the spiritual well-being, health, happiness, and safety of your children.

Follow those guidelines, not only to have happy children but because they'll make you feel better about yourself, too.

13

Time for Reform

DIVORCE has become an American institution. In some cities, the frequency of divorce almost equals that of marriage. In 1975, for instance, 16,500 marriages were performed in the Atlanta metropolitan area and 15,000 divorces were granted. Almost everyone has a friend, acquaintance, or relative who has been divorced. Although divorce may not carry the moral stigma it once had, the trauma inflicted by antiquated laws, greedy attorneys, overburdened and uncaring judges, and vindictive mates leaves indelible marks.

It is time for serious divorce reform. No-fault has been adopted in many states, but few divorce experts think it is the answer, either. More significant and effective changes must be made.

Hundreds of interviews with divorced men and women, ministers, social workers, and lawyers have convinced me that some of the following changes would represent progress toward fair and humane divorce in the United States.

Child Custody

A fundamental effort should be made to close the legal loopholes that allow parents to deprive their ex-mates of the company of their children. State laws should be enacted to prohibit one parent from taking the children out of state and away from the other parent in order to obtain a divorce in a different jurisdiction. Frequently, this is done with the deliberate intent of separating one parent from his or her children.

The means to end divorce-related kidnapping is at hand in the Uniform Child Custody Jurisdiction Act, approved by the American Bar Association in 1968. States adopting the law have agreed to respect the custody orders of other states, regardless of whether the other state has adopted the law.

At press time at least 34 states have adopted it and at least five states including Illinois, Maine, Massachusetts, and New Hampshire have it pending in their legislatures. Some child kidnapping cases in some states may now be a criminal offense if contrary to court custody. Check with your attorney.

The grounds for custody should be revised. A husband shouldn't have to prove a mother is unfit in order to obtain custody of his children. Rather, parents should have to prove individually that they are capable of rearing their children, leaving the court to decide who would do the better job.

Custody today is almost always awarded to the mother, unless she is grossly unfit. In the past, there were good economic and other reasons why mothers were awarded custody, but those reasons are largely archaic under today's conditions. Fathers should be guaranteed equal protection under the law.

If psychological testing and welfare investigations indicate neither parent is fit to take custody of the children, the children should be sent to a foster home. Children sent to these temporary homes would be removed from a dangerous or neglectful situation.

Legal Fees

Let contracting parties pay for the lawyer they engage. I feel strongly that it may be unconstitutional to require a man to pay an attorney to divide up his family and assets. A woman should pay her attorney if she has money of her own. Otherwise, her lawyer's fees should be paid out of her settlement funds.

Lawyers should be required to take a more reasonable approach to fees. They should itemize the exact hours they spend on a case and not charge by "guess-timate." All copies of legal and court documents should be available to the client for his or her personal records. In case of a change of counsel, these papers should be immediately available to the client and not held as collateral for payment of fees.

Legal insurance or installment arrangements for the payment of the legal fees would be another beneficial charge. Fees paid for a divorce should be tax deductible.

Alimony

Courts should require a periodic review of a man's financial situation so that alimony or child support payments could be reduced where there is financial hardship. Working ex-wives, as their income increases, should be required gradually to assume more of the financial burden for the support of their children. Need should be one of the most important guidelines for determining the size of alimony and child support payments. Alimony and child support should not be used as punitive devices. Excessive alimony and child support should not be granted simply to fatten the fees of rapacious attorneys.

Marriage Education

Our booming divorce rate is bad for society, but little is being done to retard it. One solution is education. More schools should teach better courses on family life to students before they are married or reach marriageable age. Such courses should stress the emotional maturity required for marriage and teach specific skills, particularly in budgeting and on personal finances. Too many marriages founder on financial problems.

Post-Divorce Counseling

As young people must be educated for marriage, opportunities for divorced persons to receive counseling should also be made available. There are too many lost souls whose lives need to be given new direction. Psychologists, psychiatrists, social workers, ministers, friends and relatives, even singles organizations can contribute to their recovery.

Legal Training and Licensing

Today, any lawyer who has passed the bar examination can practice in the emotion-laden, extremely complex field of divorce, Any judge, elected or appointed, can hear cases in marital relations court.

We should require that divorce lawyers be trained in the human relations as well as the legal aspects of divorce. We need divorce lawyers with humanity, empathy, and basic human compassion and understanding. We don't need legal butchers who thrive on splitting couples apart. And lawyers once admitted to divorce practice should be subject to review by a citizens' panel if a sufficient number of complaints are made about them. The local bar association usually can't be relied upon to deal severely with one of its members.

The Honorable Charles J. Fleck, presiding judge of the Domestic Relations Division of Cook County, Illinois, Circuit Court, feels "strongly that lawyers and judges both should have mandatory testing and retesting to update their skills, increase their knowledge of the law, and reduce incompetency. This would be good for the legal profession because it would be an improvement. It would cause the public's opinion of judges and lawyers to surge."

Divorce Information

There should be a facility that offers free information to persons experiencing marital difficulties. The American Bar Association or local bar associations could set up such information centers. They would not offer legal advice but would provide information regarding divorce laws, the procedures required to obtain a divorce, and referrals to lawyers specializing in specific areas of divorce practice. Such a referral agency also could refer warring mates to the social agencies specializing in marital and personal counseling. Generally, once a couple sees a lawyer, divorce is inevitable. An attorney is not a marriage counselor. He earns his fees by severing marriages, not saving them.

An information service where couples could learn about what is ahead of them, without being pressured to begin proceedings by an attorney, might save many a shaky marriage. This service could be a strong deterrent to the hasty decisions now being made by couples rushing into divorce.

No-Fault Divorce Legislation

Many states have recently adopted no-fault divorce legislation and others have similar laws on the drawing boards. Unfortunately, people see no-fault as a panacea. It is supposed to solve everything. It doesn't. It allows one to obtain a divorce, but then other items become the object of litigation. Fault again becomes important in deciding the division of property, child custody, and alimony. Lawyers have said that no-fault divorce is cheaper, and it may be, but the lawyers still get their share in litigation to divide property and determine alimony and child support.

A friend of mine, who is the senior law partner of a prestigious Chicago firm, suggests that the only real reform would be to have a true no-fault system. Under true no-fault, a court clerk would help a couple fill out the required papers. When the forms were completed, the couple would be divorced. It would be as simple, straightforward, and inexpensive as buying a fishing license. Property settlements and custody matters could be resolved between the couple, with the aid of a public ombudsman and a guardian ad litem, and then be approved by the courts.

The impact of no-fault on wives and children should be carefully reviewed. A recent report of the National Commission on the Observance of International Women's Year suggests that no-fault laws are having a negative economic impact on them. According to former U.S. Representative Martha Griffiths, who chaired a homemaker committee for the commission, "One 1972 nationwide study of 133 couples divorced since 1968 showed that after alimony and child support payments are made, the economic status of former husbands improves while that of former wives deteriorates."

Locating Former Spouse

If one must contact a missing ex-spouse, a letter to the spouse should be sent to: Social Security Administration, P.O. Box 57, Baltimore, Maryland 21203. This must be accompanied by a note explaining the reason for wanting to contact the spouse.

For a nominal fee there is also a Social Security Federal Locator Program for tracing ex-spouses with arrearages in support payments.

Guardian ad Litem

There should be uniform provision in all states for court appointment of an impartial guardian ad litem to act in behalf of the children. It is difficult for the attorneys representing the adversary litigants to place the welfare of the children above the welfare of their individual clients. They are being paid to represent the mother or the father, each of whom may be determined to have custody of the children. Inevitably, their effort will be to try to fulfill the wishes of the client, rather than the needs of the child. A guardian ad litem can help ensure that the child's interests are not sacrificed to the emotional needs of the parents.

Federal Law on Divorce

Some experts have suggested the enactment of a federal divorce law. It should eliminate the shopping around for the best state divorce law that still occurs because of the wide variation in divorce statutes from one state to another.

Until or unless a federal divorce statute becomes a reality, the best way to achieve more just divorces would be for the judges to administer fairly the laws now on the books. One learned lawyer told me that in his twenty years of experience, judges have tended to rule mechanistically, rather than with a real concern for justice and equality for both divorcing spouses.

A federal statute, however, is not the only way to achieve uniform divorce law in the United States. The individual states could adopt a uniform code. The code could be developed by the American Bar Association's Commission of Uniform Laws with the advice of qualified judges, lawyers, psychologists, psychiatrists, social workers, ministers, priests, rabbis and divorced persons. This has already been done in many other areas of mutual concern to all states.

What You Can Do

Divorce reform will not come, however, unless there is strong evidence of public interest and concern. Write your senator. Write your congressman and your state legislators. Give them your opinion of the gross inequities and unfairness you have observed or experienced. Let's stop being complacent because "that's the way it is." It is that way only because we let it be that way.

Let's take some of the profits out of the divorce racket. Let's get rid of the unqualified and vicious lawyers and incompetent judges. Let's get some sympathy, understanding, compassion and help for the victims of unfortunate marriages.

Because so much of the moral stigma has been removed, divorce is a growing reality. Increasingly, unhappy couples are unwilling to stay married for life, or even—as once was often the case—until their children are grown. That's not all bad because, although divorce is harmful to children, life in a tension-ridden household is often worse.

It is time, then, to move on several fronts:

- Teach married couples how to handle their marital problems.
- Develop uniformity in divorce laws and procedures.
- Bring the rapacious, unethical divorce lawyers under control.
- Soften the adversary nature of divorce proceedings.
- Provide equity for divorcing husbands and wives and, most of all, for children.

It won't be easy because the present laws are written for lawyers and will have to be changed by lawyers, who hold more than their share of legislative posts in the Congress and in legislatures across the United States. But with sufficient public outcry, it can be done.

Bibliography

Divorce

Ashman, Charles R. *The Finest Judges Money Can Buy and Other Forms of Judicial Pollution.* Los Angeles: Nash Publishing, 1973.
Exposes judicial corruption in the United States. Read a few cases to keep yourself ever mindful of the extreme latitude and discretionary power a judge has.

Black, Henry Campbell. *Black's Law Dictionary.* 4th ed. rev. St. Paul: West Publishing Co., 1968.
"The Code of Professional Responsibility" is near the front.

Blake, Nelson Manfred. *The Road To Reno.* New York: The MacMillan Co., 1962.
A history of divorce in the United States, including background on New York's divorce law and attempts to liberalize it.

Bohannan, Paul, ed. *Divorce and After.* Garden City, N.Y.: Doubleday & Co., Inc., 1970.
A collection of essays on divorce.

Boylan, Brian Richard. *Legal Rights of Women.* New York: Award Books, 1971. (paperback) London: Tandem Books, 1971.

De Benedictis, Daniel J. *Legal Rights of Married Women.* New York: Cornerstone Library, 1969. (paperback)

DeWolf, Rose. *The Bonds of Acrimony.* New York: J.B. Lippincott Co., 1970.

Points out the price of acrimony and suggests changes in the divorce laws to avoid it.

Felder, Raoul Lionel. *Divorce: The Way Things Are, Not The Way Things Should Be.* New York and Cleveland: The World Publishing Co., 1971.

A realistic discussion of the divorce experience.

Fisher, Ester Oshiver. *Divorce: The New Freedom.* New York: Harper & Row, 1974.

Written by a marriage and divorce counselor. Uses many case histories to illustrate that readers' problems are shared ones.

Frohlich, Newton. *Making The Best of It.* New York: Harper & Row, 1971.

Common-sense advice on negotiation as a substitute for recrimination.

Gershenson, Alvin H. *The Bench Is Warped.* New York, Washington, Hollywood: Vantage Press, 1963.

An inside look at legal injustice. Read in particular Chap. 15, pp. 158-168, "Can You Spot Your Enemy?"

Gettlemen, Susan, and Janet Markowitz. *The Courage To Divorce.* New York: Simon and Schuster, 1974.

Divorce, according to the authors, can be positive and liberating—under certain conditions.

Hirsch, Barbara B. *Divorce: What A Woman Needs to Know.* Chicago: Henry Regnery Co., 1973. (paperback)

Information about procedures, grounds, defenses, custody, and support questions and answers, written especially for women.

Kelleher, Stephen J. *Divorce and Remarriage for Catholics.* Garden City: Doubleday & Co., Inc., 1973.

Discussion of marriage and divorce and information about annulment.

Metz, Charles V. *Divorce and Custody for Men.* Garden City: Doubleday & Co., Inc., 1968.

Especially recommended for men who want to learn how to fight.

Nizer. Louis. *My Life In Court.* Garden City: Doubleday & Co., Inc., 1961.

Chapter 2 is on divorce. Insight on divorce and lawyers in general.

Pospishil, Victor J. *Divorce in The Progressive Area.* New York: Herder & Herder, 1967.
Catholic teachings about divorce and marriage.

Rodell, John S. *How To Avoid Alimony.* New York: Stein & Day, 1969.

Rosenblatt, Stanley. *The Divorce Racket.* Los Angeles: Nash Publishing Corp., 1969.
The author discusses defenses and grounds for divorce, adversaries, the tremendous power and discretion of judges, alimony, abuses, and changes suggested for improvements.

Sheresky, Norman, and Marya Mannes. *Uncoupling: The Art of Coming Apart.* New York: The Viking Press, 1972.
Good advice on the selection of lawyers.

Sherwin, Robert Veit. *Compatible Divorce.* New York: Crown Publishers, Inc., 1969.
A discussion of ways to remove acrimony from divorce.

Steinzor, Bernard. *When Parents Divorce: A New Approach to New Relationships.* New York: Pantheon Books, 1969.
A psychologist's guidelines to help couples achieve greater understanding.

Tax Planning In Divorce & Separation. Chicago: Commerce Clearing House, 1975.
This 1975 booklet may help resolve tax questions.

Wheeler, Michael Allen. *No-Fault Divorce.* Boston: Beacon Press, 1974.

Post-Divorce Problems

Athearn, Louise Montague. *What Every Formerly Married Woman Should Know.* New York: David McKay Co., Inc., 1973.
Questions and answers for women trying to adjust to being single again.

Baer, Jean. *The Second Wife.* Garden City: Doubleday & Co., Inc., 1972.
Baer brings her experience as a second wife to the reader, along with information derived from 200 interviews of second wives.

Bernard, Jessie. *Remarriage: A Study of Marriage.* New York: Russell & Russell, 1956 (reissued 1971).
A study of divorce and remarriage.

Block, Jean Libman. *Back in Circulation*. London: Collier-MacMillan, Ltd., 1969.
Advice on how to become a single woman again.

Egleson, Jim and Janet Frank Egleson. *Parents Without Partners*. New York: Ace Books, Inc., 1961. (paperback)
Guidance for divorced, separated, and widowed parents in dea ing with children.

Evans, Louis H. *Your Marriage: Duel or Duet?* Old Tappan, N. J.: Fleming H. Revell Co., 1972.
Louis Evans is a successful pastor, experienced in the craft of marriage counseling. This is a practical book that includes commonsense advice on how to create rewarding partnership in marriage.

Freda, Dorothy Marie. *Love: The Second Time Around*. New York: Laddin Press, 1969.
The author, a young widow, has written a compassionate guide for the single-again woman that gives honest advice on how to start living again, laughing again, and, most important, loving again.

Hunt, Morton M. *The World of The Formerly Married*. New York: McGraw-Hill Book Co., 1966.
Highly recommended book on the reactions of divorced and separated persons.

Krantzler, Mel. *Creative Divorce: A New Opportunity for Personal Growth*. New York: M. Evans and Co., Inc., 1974.
More advice on adjusting to single life.

Mindey, Carol. *The Divorced Mother*. New York: McGraw-Hill Book Co., 1969.
The author, a divorced mother, relates with candor and good humor what did and did not work for her and offers sensible advice on how to overcome the emotional stresses that accompany divorce.

Rohner, Louise. *The Divorcee's Handbook*. New York: Doubleday & Co., Inc., 1967.
Records the author's experience and explains how any divorcee can reestablish a rewarding life, with or without a new mate.

Waller, Willard. *The Old Love and The New*. London: Feffer and Simons, Inc., 1930, 1967.
In this original study, Waller shifted the focus from divorce as a social problem to divorce as an event in an individual's life history. This work is a forerunner in the field of divorce.

Divorce and Children

Atkon, Edith, and Estelle Rubin. *Part-Time Father.* New York: The Vanguard Press, Inc., 1976.

Advice for fathers on visitation with their children. Problems common to many are discussed.

Despert, Louise J., M.D. *Children of Divorce.* Garden City: Doubleday & Co., Inc., 1953.

A child psychiatrist offers practical advice to parents who are divorcing, using case studies.

Gardner, Richard A., M.D. *The Boys and Girls Book About Divorce.* Scranton: Science House, Inc., 1970.

An excellent guide to help parents explain divorce to children, and how to relieve anxieties. Illustrated.

Goff, Beth. *Where Is Daddy? The Story of a Divorce.* Boston: Beacon Press, 1969.

Grollman, Earl A. *Explaining Divorce to Children.* Boston: Beacon Press, 1969.

Stuart, Irving R., and Lawrence E. Abt. *Children of Separation and Divorce.* New York: Grossman Publishers, 1972.

Advice on how to make divorce easier for children.